DR. HISTORY'S
WHIZZ-BANG

Favorite Stories
of California's Past
by
Jim Rawls

Edited by
Leonard Nelson and
Denise Culver Nelson

Illustrations by
Andrea Hendrick

t

Tioga Publishing Company
Palo Alto, California

Illustrations and Cover Design   *Andrea Hendrick*
Interior Design   *Jennifer Ballentine*
Copyediting   *Geri Jeter*
Proofreading   *Kathleen McClung*
Text Programming   *Bruce Boston*
Electronic Composition   *Professional Book Center*

Rawls, James J.
    Dr. History's whizz-bang : favorite stories of California's past /
by Jim Rawls
        p.   cm.
    Includes bibliographic references and index.
    Summary: A collection of light-hearted stories from California's
past, bringing out aspects of the state's history, geography,
culture, and ethnicity.
    ISBN 0-935382-77-1 : $9.95
    1. California History—History—Juvenile literature.   [1. California—
History.]   I. Title.   II. Title: Doctor History's whizz-bang.
F861.3.R39   1991
979.4—dc20   91-27640
                                                            CIP
                                                            AC

Printed in the United States of America by Malloy Lithographers

Tioga Publishing Company
P.O. Box 50490
Palo Alto CA 94303
415-965-4081

FOREWORD

Frank Dill and Mike Cleary
Morning Radio Hosts KNBR 68, San Francisco

lot of people think history is dull. It's always been associated with memorizing dry facts and dates. This is not
true of Dr. History, a.k.a. Professor Jim Rawls of Diablo
Valley College. We discovered that Jim has the ability to
breathe life into a story, making history fun to hear. He doesn't just
make history interesting, unusual, and bizarre, he shows us that history *is*, in fact, interesting, unusual, and bizarre. Simply put, he
knows how to tell a great story.

Jim Rawls, "The Man Who Makes History Fun" as we like to
say on the radio, teaches us that history is right at our feet. He can
always find a story somewhere near our home, work, school, or the
street corner we pass everyday. Mike learned that down the hill from
his Piedmont home is the site of Gertrude Stein's ten-acre Oakland
farm where she spent her childhood. And Frank was surprised to
hear that Marin County's Strawberry Point, a place he has passed for
many years on his way to work, was once considered for the permanent home of the United Nations.

As radio listeners across Northern California get ready for
work and school, Jim tells his stories of early California. His fan mail
reveals that Dr. History is as popular with our younger listeners as he
is with their moms and dads. He is a radio history instructor who
gets a lesson in before the school bell even rings.

Since we're not only entertained by his stories, but are also
learning something about the Golden State's past, we decided to
adopt Jim as our show's official history teacher! We even take his
history exams on the air, knowing that we are testing ourselves
along with our listeners.

Now Dr. History has collected his favorite stories in a book.
A word of caution, however, about picking up *Dr. History's Whizz-
Bang*: The stories are so fascinating the book becomes irresistible
and hard to put down. When a story comes to an end, you can't
help but turn the page to peek at the next one. Once you've looked,
you're hooked on another story!

This is a multipurpose book. The *Whizz-Bang* is mainly for browsing, to pick up again and again when you have a few minutes to read. But you can also use the book as a handy touring guide to California's many historical sites listed in the "Something More" section found at the end of each story. It's a terrific reference book and memory aid to the stories Jim tells on the air, and you will dazzle your friends with your historical expertise straight from Dr. History.

The *Whizz-Bang* is also a great storybook for children. Frank knows his grandkids love to have stories read to them at bedtime, and Dr. History's book is both fun and educational. Mike feels the same way, but instead of reading the stories to his kids, he's going to give the *Whizz-Bang* to his wife and have her read bedtime stories to him!

Before we get back to our *Whizz-Bangs*, we want to remind you that Professor Jim's book is truly entertaining for the whole family. OK, now it's your turn. Can you tell us why there are camel barns in Benicia? (No peeking.) Give up? Read the *Whizz-Bang*!

Frank Dill

Mike Cleary
Morning Radio Hosts KNBR 68, San Francisco

KNBR 68
SAN FRANCISCO

WELCOME

ust what is a "whizz-bang"? My only other encounter with this rather curious term was in the lyrics to the song "Ya Got Trouble," from Meredith Willson's hit musical, *The Music Man*. One of the signs of "trouble in River City," sings Professor Harold Hill to worried Iowa parents, is that their children are starting to "memorize jokes from *Captain Billy's Whiz Bang*." As it turns out, this earlier "whizz-bang" was a wildly popular, early twentieth-century, pocket-size magazine specializing in earthy illustrations and humor. Like its namesake, *Dr. History's Whizz-Bang* trades in out-of-the-way stories, but this time about the famous, and not-so-famous, heroes of California history.

On behalf of the California Historical Society, it is a great personal pleasure to welcome readers to this delightful book by teacher, writer, and master story-teller Jim Rawls. Like the fascinating tales he weaves, Jim's involvement with the California Historical Society goes back a long way. Since he received his doctorate in history from the University of California, Berkeley, Jim Rawls has helped the Society to build awareness of the state's exciting heritage, a work he continues to this day. For his invaluable contributions over nearly two decades, the California Historical Society recently honored Jim by designating him a "Fellow," an award reserved for distinguished historians.

Jim Rawls is dedicated to the belief that history is not confined to arid texts and isolated classrooms, but is a vital adventure of human intelligence and imagination from which all people can gain insight and entertainment. With the assistance of radio producer Leonard Nelson, Jim has collected for this book his favorite stories from the "Dr. History" feature on KNBR's "Frank & Mike Show." Through its pages you enter the always intriguing, sometimes quirky, world of California history and mystery.

Those who like good stories will find even more of them at the California Historical Society. Designated by the legislature as the official state historical society, the California Historical Society sponsors lectures, tours, exhibits, and school activities around the state and publishes *California History*, a quarterly magazine of articles and reviews, and the *California Chronicle*, a newsletter of statewide historical events. The California Historical Society encourages you to take advantage of its varied programs, just as it welcomes you to the captivating pages of *Dr. History's Whizz-Bang*.

Richard J. Orsi
Editor of California History:
The Magazine of the California Historical Society

ACKNOWLEDGMENTS

any talented and generous people have helped make this book possible. I am especially grateful to Marlene Smith-Baranzini, a fellow California historian who has done much of the basic research for many of Dr. History's favorite stories. Her dedication and enthusiasm have been sustaining.

Likewise Dr. Phyllis L. Peterson, President of Diablo Valley College, has been the source of unfailing encouragement and goodwill. Grant Cooke, the Public Relations Officer for Diablo Valley College, has also been a faithful supporter of Dr. History.

Several individuals at the California Historical Society deserve special thanks: Michael McCone, Executive Director; Richard J. Orsi, editor of *California History*; and Cheryl Kolinen, Director of Development.

I am also grateful to KNBR 68 for the opportunity to share a few good California stories on the radio. Most notably I want to thank Tony Salvadore, Vice President and General Manager of KNBR; Dwight Walker, Manager/Station Administrator; and Bob Agnew, Program Director. Thanks especially to the costars of the "Dr. History Show," Frank Dill and Mike Cleary. They've been the best perpetual students I've ever had the pleasure of teaching. (And thanks too, fellows, for all those shiny apples around exam time!)

At KNBR my biggest debt of gratitude is to Leonard Nelson, producer of the "Frank & Mike Show" and the creator of "Dr. History." It was Leonard's idea to air the feature on KNBR and to turn the stories into a book. He and his coconspirator, Denise Culver Nelson, have put in countless hours to make this enterprise a success.

CONTENTS

THE GREAT CALIFORNIA HEALTH RUSH

Everybody knows about the California gold rush, but did you know there was also a California health rush back in the late 1800s? Thousands of people rushed to California believing that just being in the Golden State would somehow cure all kinds of ailments. There was a consumption and rheu-

matism rush in the 1870s and 1880s, although I'm not too sure folks with rheumatism really could do much "rushing!"

Railroads and real estate promoters, anxious to sell tickets or property to those hopeful newcomers, carefully nourished belief in the health-giving properties of California. Some of their claims were pretty far out, and unfortunately they left a lot of folks bitterly disappointed and disillusioned.

Communities up and down California all wanted a piece of the action. One resort in the Napa Valley claimed that drinking its "California mineral waters" would cure everything from gout to diseases of the "bladder, womb, and ear." An outfit near Walnut Creek invited folks to come bathe in their pools of "sulphur spring waters" and experience the miracle of their "magical medicinal curative powers."

Even the city of Oakland jumped on the bandwagon and billed itself as "Oakland: Health City." One brochure claimed that "according to unimpeachable statistics, Oakland is the healthiest city in the country." Not to be outdone, cities in the Central Valley also began to promote their alleged healthfulness. Potential newcomers to Stockton and Visalia were advised that these two cities "are most favorable for consumptives and persons subject to throat difficulties."

Several attempts were made in the late 1800s to document whether Californians truly were more healthy than other Americans. Probably the most famous of these was a study described by the biologist David Starr Jordan, the first president of Stanford University. Around 1900 President Jordan reported on a scientific study that compared the "bodily dimensions" of coeds on a college campus in Massachusetts with the physical proportions of coeds in California. (I've always been curious about the research methods used in this intriguing study.) The results, President Jordan claimed, showed clearly that the California coeds were superior physical specimens:

> California college girls, of the same age, are larger by almost every dimension than are the college girls of Massachusetts. They are taller, broader-shouldered, thicker-chested (with ten cubic inches more lung capacity), have larger biceps and calves, and a superiority of tested strength.

Oh, those California girls!

❧ Something More ... *View the marvelous collection of late nineteenth century promotional materials on display at the Oakland Museum, 1000 Oak Street, at the corner of Tenth and Oak streets, Oakland 94607. Free. Hours are 10:00 A.M. to 5:00 P.M. Wednesday through Saturday, and 12:00 P.M. to 7:00 P.M. Sunday. Telephone (415) 273-3401. For an entertaining account of the Great California Health Rush, see John E. Baur,* Health Seekers of Southern California *(1959). Other more general accounts may be found in Glenn S. Dumke,* The Boom of the Eighties *(1944) and Kevin Starr,* Inventing the Dream: California through the Progressive Era *(1985).*

NO HONEYMOON FOR BELLE CORA

elle Cora, née Arabella Ryan, was one of the most notorious ladies of the California frontier. She was the beautiful mistress of San Francisco gambler Charles Cora and a very successful business woman in her own right. She owned and managed two parlor houses in the city and by 1853 was probably the wealthiest madam in San Francisco.

All was going well for Belle until one evening in 1855 when she and Charles decided to attend the theater. Unfortunately for them, they were seated directly behind William H. Richardson, a United States marshal, and his wife. Mrs. Richardson considered herself a proper lady and took offense at Belle's presence. After the Richardsons complained to the theater manager, they stormed out in a rage.

A couple of days later, Marshal Richardson and Charles Cora happened to run into each other in a saloon on Clay Street. They got into a heated argument about the theater incident and apparently reached an impasse. Charles finished the conversation by pulling out a derringer and shooting the marshal dead!

Charles Cora was tried for murder, but Belle, resourceful as ever, retained a brilliant trial lawyer, hired witnesses, and bribed the jury. Not surprisingly, Charles was acquitted. The good people of San Francisco were outraged by this obvious miscarriage of justice and formed a Vigilance Committee. They seized Charles Cora, retried him, and sentenced him to hang. As he waited to die, Charles was granted one last request. A priest was allowed to visit the condemned man. Then, just moments before Charles was executed, he and his beloved Belle were wed.

As a "newlywed widow," Belle Cora continued to live the luxurious life of a grieving but high-priced madam. Before her death in 1862, she arranged to be buried next to Charles in the cemetery at Mission Dolores. Their graves were marked by a stone sculpture of a couple in deep mourning, she holding a bouquet and he with his

EXECUTION OF JAMES P. CASEY AND CHARLES CORA,
BY THE VIGILANCE COMMITTEE, OF SAN FRANCISCO,
On Thursday, May 22d, 1856, from the Windows of their Rooms, in Sacramento Street, between Front and Davis Streets.

hat grasped in one hand, each reaching out pitifully toward the weeping branches of a tree. The sculpture has long since been removed, but the headstones of Charles and Belle remain as silent monuments to the briefest marriage in San Francisco's long and colorful past.

> ❧ *Something More* ... *Visit the graves of Belle and Charles Cora in the cemetery of Mission Dolores, corner of 16th and Dolores streets, San Francisco 94114. Donation. Hours are 9:00 A.M. to 4:00 P.M. daily. Telephone (415) 621-8203. Their story can also be found in Jacqueline Barnhart,* The Fair but Frail: Prostitutes in San Francisco, 1849–1900 *(1986).*

CAMELS IN CALIFORNIA?

mporting camels to California was the bright idea of an imaginative young senator from Mississippi named Jefferson Davis. He was convinced that camels—famous for their sure-footedness in shifting sands and their ability to endure intense heat—would be an ideal means of transporting military supplies to California through the deserts of the American southwest. After Davis became United States Secretary of War in 1853, he dispatched government agents to northern Africa to purchase a small herd of camels. The camels eventually arrived in New Mexico where they were assigned the task of transporting goods over a twelve-hundred-mile desert trail to California.

On their maiden voyage west, the camels averaged twenty-five miles a day and finished their trek in about fifty days. The caravan arrived safely in California without losing a single man or beast. Some of the soldiers who served as camel tenders did complain that the rolling gait of their ungainly mounts had made them seasick. Others said that the camels had extremely rude manners. When angry or upset, the discomfited dromedaries had the unpleasant habit of ejecting their cuds into the faces of unsuspecting onlookers!

Although the camel experiment was a practical success, it proved to be a political failure. With the advent of the Civil War in 1861, funding for this innovative transportation scheme dried up. The camels also had the misfortune of being associated with Jefferson Davis, by then serving as President of the Confederacy, an association not calculated to win the camels many friends in the Union Congress.

In the early 1860s, some thirty-five hapless camels were driven north from Los Angeles to the army's Benicia Arsenal in the East Bay and auctioned off to the highest bidder. Years later, sun-baked prospectors claimed to have sighted petrified camel pies and herds of feral camels galumphing across the desert sands. Such sightings have never been substantiated and probably should be put down as tall tale rather than historical fact.

❧ Something More … *Visit the former residence of the California camels, the Benicia Camel Barns, 2024 Camel Road, Benicia 94510. A $1.00 donation for admission is suggested. Hours are 1:00 P.M. to 4:00 P.M. Saturday and Sunday. Telephone (707) 745-5435. Annual camel races are held each February at the Riverside County National Date Festival, Desert ExpoCentre, 46350 Arabia Street, Indio 92201. Telephone (619) 342-8247.*

BLOOD BROTHERS
AT THE *CHRONICLE*

any northern Californians begin each day with a familiar routine—gulping down a cup of steaming hot coffee while thumbing through the pages of their morning newspaper, the *San Francisco Chronicle*. Founded in 1865 by two teenage brothers, Charles and M. H. de Young, the paper began as a giveaway, four-page theater guide called the *Daily Dramatic Chronicle*. The de Youngs expanded the publication into a regular daily newspaper after successfully scooping their rivals at the end of the Civil War by being the first paper in the city to report the assassination of Abraham Lincoln. Shades of things to come.

The de Young brothers were combative, hard-hitting editors. In 1879, Charles de Young published a bitter, personal attack on a candidate for the office of mayor of San Francisco. The candidate, a Baptist minister named Isaac Kalloch, retaliated by denouncing de Young from his pulpit. De Young was so outraged that he drove over to Kalloch's church and demanded to see the minister. When Reverend Kalloch approached de Young's carriage, de Young pulled out a derringer and shot him. Kalloch survived the attempted assassination and won the election. Soon afterward, the newly elected mayor's son revenged the assault on his father by visiting the editorial offices of the *Chronicle* and fatally shooting Charles de Young!

Four years after Charles's death, M. H. de Young became embroiled in a similar battle with Adolph Spreckels, the head of the great San Francisco sugar refining company. M. H. published an editorial charging that Spreckels had defrauded his stockholders, which so infuriated Spreckels that he paid a visit to de Young and shot and seriously wounded him.

M. H. de Young and Adolph Spreckels lived for many more years and both became great patrons of the city of San Francisco. In 1916, de Young established the art museum in Golden Gate Park that now bears his name. Not to be outdone, eight years later,

A BEASTLY PRIEST BECOMES A PRIESTLY DEMAGOGUE

THE SLIMY TRAIL OF THE REV. I. S. KALLOCH

from MAINE to CALIFORNIA.

LOST HIS WAY "I AIN'T DONE NOTHIN'"

Adolph Spreckels donated his own fine arts museum to the city, the Palace of the Legion of Honor, located in Lincoln Park.

Ironically, in 1972 the de Young Museum merged with the Palace of the Legion of Honor to form the Fine Arts Museums of San Francisco. Two men who were mortal enemies in life are now joined in death by the merging of their two great gifts to the city they loved.

> **🍃 Something More** ... *Visit the M. H. de Young Museum in San Francisco's Golden Gate Park, 94118, and the Palace of the Legion of Honor, corner of 34th and Clement streets in Lincoln Park, 94121. Admission for both museums is adults $4.00, students and seniors $2.00. Hours are 10:00 A.M. to 5:00 P.M. Wednesday through Sunday. Telephone (415) 750-3600. The dramatic story of early San Francisco journalism is well told in John Roberts Bruce,* Gaudy Century *(1948).*

Rodeo, Cornmeal, and Little Hill Hill

hile driving along Interstate 80 in Contra Costa County, consider the origins of the names Rodeo, Pinole, and El Cerrito. The word "rodeo" (pronounced ro-DAY-oh) first appeared on a land grant in Contra Costa back when California was still part of Mexico. Of course, a rodeo in Mexican California was a far cry from the circus-like weekend entertainment, the RO-dee-oh, we're familiar with today. The original rodeos were busy roundups where range animals were sorted out and branded by Mexican cowhands.

Whenever I pass through Rodeo, I'm always reminded how much of our American cowboy heritage is really Hispanic. Not only is "rodeo" Spanish in origin, so too is "bronco," which means wild or untamed. The cowboy's "lariat" comes from the Spanish *la riata* meaning rope. Even the term "buckaroo" comes from the Spanish. It's a corruption of the word "vaquero" (pronounced vah-CARE-oh) which is Spanish for cowhand. Remember the term "calaboose" from TV westerns? This too comes from the Spanish, *calabozo*, meaning dungeon or prison cell.

A little south of Rodeo is the town of Pinole. The word "pinole" is an Aztec term meaning cornmeal. It was later hispanicized and applied to any kind of ground meal, including the Native American diet of ground acorns and wild grass seeds. Apparently, the name was first applied to the present-day site in Contra Costa County in 1775 when a group of Spanish soldiers passed through the area and were given some kind of gruel or porridge by the local Indians. Hence they named the place Pinole.

Then there's El Cerrito. Originally the town had the rather prosaic name of County Line because it was situated near the line between Alameda and Contra Costa counties. Things improved slightly in the early 1900s when, for a time, it was known as "the city of Rust"—named after an early postmaster in the area, Mr. William Rust.

Eventually the townfolk settled on the name El Cerrito, which they took from the nearby hill that today we call Albany Hill. The Spanish had named the hill *El Cerrito*, meaning hillock or little hill, but when the Americans arrived in the area they began calling it El Cerrito Hill. The residents of nearby Rust argued they had a better claim to the name than the hill did since El Cerrito Hill was really a rather embarrassing redundancy, meaning as it did "the little hill hill." So it was that the name shifted from hill to town and all was well well.

> 🐾 ***Something More*** ... *Read Edward Staniford,* El Cerrito Historical Evolution *(1977) which can be found at the El Cerrito Public Library, 6510 Stockton Avenue, El Cerrito 94530. Also browse through Barbara and Rudy Marinacci,* California's Spanish Place-Names *(1988).*

IN PURSUIT OF FANNY

One of the greatest love stories in California history is the story of Robert Louis Stevenson's pursuit of the woman he loved. Stevenson was born in 1850 to a prosperous, middle-class family in Scotland. As a young man he was something of a nonconformist, wearing outlandish clothing and shoulder-length hair. His parents wanted him to settle down and take up a respectable career in engineering or law, but Stevenson rebelled and went to France where he fell in with a Bohemian crowd...and fell in love with Fanny Van de Grift Osbourne, an unhappily married American woman. Fanny was small, dark, and passionate. A friend once said that her black eyes were irresistible, "full of sex and mystery." Apparently Stevenson found them so, for he and Fanny had a torrid affair.

When Fanny returned to the United States with her feckless husband, the parting nearly broke Stevenson's heart. In 1879, he sailed for New York, crossed the continent to California, and found Fanny living in Monterey where the two lovers resumed their affair. After Fanny was granted a divorce, she and Stevenson were married in the spring of 1880.

The newlyweds went north to Silverado in Napa County for their honeymoon. At that time, Silverado wasn't the lavish golf and tennis resort we know today. The happy couple stayed in an empty shack near an abandoned silver mine on the slopes of Mount St. Helena. There was no room service in their lonely honeymoon cabin, and poison oak grew through the broken floor boards. But the Stevensons didn't seem to mind; they stayed at their mountain-side retreat for two months of nuptial bliss.

Stevenson's brief rendezvous in California had an important influence on his later writing career. His most successful California book, *The Silverado Squatters* (1883), is filled with delightful scenes of Napa Valley vineyards and wineries. The California countryside appears in some of his other books as well. The landscape of *Treasure Island* (1881) is a combination of scenes in Monterey County and Napa Valley, and Spyglass Hill is unmistakably Mount St. Helena!

Stevenson always regarded his time on Mount St. Helena with his bride as among the happiest days in his life. "To live out of doors with the woman one loves is of all lives," he later wrote, "the most complete and free."

> ❧ **Something More** ... *Visit the Silverado Museum at 1490 Library Lane, St. Helena 94574, and view its fine collection of Stevenson books, manuscripts, and memorabilia. Free. Hours are 12:00 P.M. to 4:00 P.M. Tuesday through Sunday. Telephone (707) 963-3757. The site of Stevenson's cabin is marked by a granite monument on a short trail from the St. Helena Crest Highway within the Robert Louis Stevenson State Park on the slopes of Mt. St. Helena. The best book on Stevenson's California sojourn is James D. Hart (ed.), From Scotland to Silverado (1966).*

KESKYDEES

alifornia is, and always has been, a land of great ethnic diversity. Throughout its history, the Golden State has attracted people from around the world. Among those who have contributed to the amalgam of California culture are the French.

The first Frenchman to visit California arrived over two hundred years ago. Jean François Galaup de La Pérouse visited California in 1786 as part of a worldwide commercial and scientific tour. However, it wasn't until the California gold rush that people from France began to arrive in California in great numbers. By 1853, a French-language newspaper in San Francisco estimated there were some thirty-two thousand French argonauts in the state. Throughout the Gold Country today are place names reminding us of this early French presence—names such as French Camp, French Corral, and French Gulch.

The French, like many other foreigners in the gold rush, raised the ire of Anglo-Americans who weren't in any mood to share the gold with those who came from other lands. The Americans derided the French by calling them "Keskydees," from the Frenchmen's frequent and uncomprehending question, *"Qu'est-ce qu'il dit?"* meaning "What does he say?"

Americans also tried to rid the state of foreign miners by requiring them to pay a special monthly tax of twenty dollars for the privilege of mining in California. The French, along with the Mexicans and some Germans, mobilized opposition to the tax and staged an unarmed protest in Sonora in 1850. Their protest came to be known as "The French Revolution."

In spite of these rough beginnings, the French stayed and succeeded in a variety of enterprises. French entrepreneurs founded some of the earliest department stores in San Francisco. In 1850, Emile Verdier brought in a shipload of Paris gowns, bonnets, laces, and silks and established the City of Paris department store on San Francisco's Union Square. Likewise, Jean Louis Vignes brought over some Bordeaux grape cuttings from his native France in 1831 and

built the first commercial winery in California. Later he was joined by other French winemakers such as Charles LeFranc of the Almaden vineyards near Los Gatos and Paul Masson in nearby Saratoga.

What could be more San Franciscan than sourdough French bread? This, too, was a French contribution to California culture, brought over during the gold rush. Sourdough was an instant hit. Miners could carry their fermented sourdough starters wherever they went. Lacking ovens, they would mix up some dough, wrap it around a stick, and bake it over their campfire. For many a lonesome miner, this was down-home cooking at its best. Hey, Keskydee, pass the biscuits, *s'il vous plait*!

&❧ **Something More** ... *Read an interesting overview of the French interest in California, Abraham P. Nasatir,* French Activities in California *(1945).*

BLACK BART

lack Bart was one of California's most colorful desperadoes. He seemed almost invincible during the 1870s and 1880s, yet he never quite lived up to the stereotypical image of a bad man of the Old West. Black Bart was a short, balding stage coach robber who didn't even own a horse and whose shotgun was so rusty it wouldn't fire. He approached his victims wearing a long linen coat and a white flour sack over his head.

Black Bart certainly had a strange modus operandi. His identifying trademarks included stealing only the money boxes of Wells Fargo stages and never robbing or harming the passengers. Instead of a trail of blood, he left behind verses of poetry signed with the name "Black Bart, the PO8."

Typical of the verses he left behind were these:

Here I lay me down to sleep
To wait the coming morrow
Perhaps success, perhaps defeat
And everlasting sorrow.

But come what may I'll try it on
My condition can't be worse
If there's munny in that Box
T'is munny in my purse.

Quite understandably, the folks at Wells Fargo were determined to catch Black Bart since he made them look like such fools. They began bolting their money boxes to the stage coach floors, hoping to slow him down.

In 1883, following his twenty-eighth successful stage coach robbery, the law finally caught up with Black Bart. In his haste to leave the scene of the crime, the highwayman accidentally dropped one of his handkerchiefs. Detectives traced the hanky to a San Francisco laundry and, from there, to its owner, one Charles E. Bolton. Bolton turned out to be a quiet, well-educated gentleman who often went into the hills on mining business. His home in San Francisco was across the street from a police station where he often dined. The

officers later recalled that the neighborly Mr. Bolton seemed to enjoy their company, particularly whenever the conversation turned to the infamous "Black Bart case."

Charles E. Bolton confessed to that one last crime and was sentenced to six years in San Quentin. After a few years behind bars, he was released. Wells Fargo tried to keep tabs on Bolton for a while, but eventually he slipped away. To the chagrin of Wells Fargo, Black Bart again surfaced and pulled off at least one final stage coach robbery before vanishing forever. His fate still remains one of the great unsolved mysteries in California history.

> ₰ *Something More* …*Visit the beautifully appointed Wells Fargo History Museum, 420 Montgomery Street, San Francisco 94163. Free. Hours are 9:00 A.M. to 5:00 P.M. Monday through Friday (excluding bank holidays). Telephone (415) 396-2619. Read the full story of Black Bart in Joseph Henry Jackson,* Bad Company *(1949). For many stories of Wells Fargo's stagecoach era, read the entertaining biography of detective James B. Hume by Richard Dillon,* Wells Fargo Detective *(1969).*

OAKLAND IS WHERE WHERE?

alifornia writer Gertrude Stein is probably best known today for her grand redundancy, "A rose is a rose is a rose is a rose." The Steins moved to Oakland in 1880 when Gertrude was just six years old. Her father was an executive with a San Francisco street car company, and the Stein family lived very comfortably in the "rural suburb" of Oakland on a ten-acre farm along 13th Avenue.

Gertrude Stein later became an expatriate living in Paris, part of that famous circle of artists and writers which included Picasso, Matisse, and Ernest Hemingway. She lived there with her longtime companion, Alice B. Toklas, a fellow writer and native San Franciscan. Stein and Toklas returned to California in 1934, spending some of their time in the East Bay trying to find Gertrude's old childhood home in Oakland.

Stein's visit to Oakland prompted her to write later that she had found no "there there," an enigmatic line which has haunted the city ever since. But Stein did not mean what most folks assume—that there's nothing very exciting about Oakland. She actually was trying to describe the experience of returning to her old neighborhood, years after leaving it, to find that nothing there was as she remembered. The "there" of her memory simply didn't exist any longer in the "there" of present-day reality. The old family farm of her childhood had vanished; the farmhouse had been torn down and replaced by rows of stucco tract housing. Her comment on Oakland was simply a comment on the rapid pace of urbanization.

Her remarks on Oakland appear in *Everybody's Biography* (1937), in which she describes going to look for the old farmhouse. But it wasn't there. She wrote, "The house, the big house and the big garden and the eucalyptus trees and the rose hedge…were not any longer existing…" Stein was left with a feeling of despair. "What was the use of my having come from Oakland," she concluded, "it was not natural to have come from there yes, write about if I like or anything if I like but not there, there is no there there."

&5 Something More ... *Visit the site of Gertrude Stein's girlhood home near the intersection of 13th Avenue and 25th Street in East Oakland and try to imagine the area as it once was. An account of Stein's early years appears in John Malcolm Brinnin,* The Third Rose: Gertrude Stein and Her World *(1987).*

RUSSIANS IN THE GOLDEN STATE

rom the perspective of most Americans, the Russians are a people who inhabit a distant land far across the Atlantic, but residents of the West Coast see things a bit differently. We know that the Russians are our next-door neighbors, a people whose eastern-most border lies just fifty-one miles across the Bering Strait from our western-most continental state.

Because of their relative proximity, Russians have long played a prominent role in California history. The fear of a Russian advance southward from the Aleutians was partly responsible for the Spanish decision to settle California in 1769. In subsequent years, Russian sea otter hunters made regular visits to the waters off the California coast. Hoping to establish diplomatic and commercial relations with the Spanish, Count Nikolai Rezanov of the Russian-American company visited San Francisco in 1806. During his visit, he ended up establishing relations of a different sort with the fifteen-year-old daughter of the San Francisco *comandante*! But that's another story.

Six years after Rezanov's visit, the Russians established an outpost north of Bodega Bay in what is now Sonoma County. Fort Ross (poetically named for the motherland, *Rossiya*) was a base for hunters in ocean-going kayaks who stalked sea otters along the California coast. It was a lucrative business. The Russians shipped the otter pelts to Russia or China where they fetched as much as three hundred dollars each. The trade was not such a good deal, of course, from the otters' point of view. They were hunted to near extinction. In 1839, the Russians deemed the harvest complete and abandoned Fort Ross.

Other reminders of the early Russian presence in California are the Russian River in Sonoma County and Russian Hill in San Francisco. The Russians originally named the river the *Slavianka*, meaning "Slav Woman," an appelation that reveals much about what was on the minds of those lonely otter hunters in California! Later the Spanish renamed the river *El Rio Ruso*, translated in turn by American settlers as "Russian River." Russian Hill in San Francisco was so named because several Russian sea-otter hunters lie buried near its summit. (The exact location of their graves was discovered recently during an excavation at the corner of Jones and Vallejo streets.)

Russian visitors were not always welcomed by the Spanish in California. Officially the Spanish regarded the Russians at Fort Ross as trespassers on Spanish soil. Nevertheless, there was no way the Spanish could force the Russians to leave. The weakness of the Spanish position was graphically illustrated one day when a Russian ship sailed into San Francisco Bay. As the ship passed by the Presidio, it fired a salute to the Spanish flag. The salute was not returned. The Russians soon saw a small boat approaching from shore. When the boat reached the ship, the Spanish officer on board sheepishly explained that only one of his cannon was safe to fire and, even so, it was completely out of gunpowder. If the Russians would be so kind as to loan some gunpowder, he concluded, he would be most happy to return the Russian salute. Had this been a hostile encounter, it is highly unlikely the Russians would have complied with this neighborly request!

> *Something More* ... *Visit the restored buildings and Visitors Center at Fort Ross State Park, 19005 Coast Highway 1, Fort Ross 95450, approximately twelve miles north of Jenner. Admission $5.00. Hours are 10:00 A.M. to 4:30 P.M. daily. Telephone (707) 847-3286. Two comprehensive histories of the Russians in California are James R. Gibson,* Imperial Russia in Frontier America *(1976) and P. A. Tikhmenev,* A History of the Russian-American Company *(1978).*

HUMORISTS OF THE COMSTOCK

y favorite western humorist is a fellow who is all but forgotten today. His name was William Wright. He wrote for the Virginia City *Territorial Enterprise* in the heyday of the Comstock silver boom. Like many writers in those days, Wright adopted various pen names. For a while he was known as Ebenezer Queerkutt and Picaroon Pax, but eventually he settled on the nom de plume of Dan De Quille for his "dandy quill."

Dan's early colleague in Virginia City was a young humorist named Samuel Clemens, who first used the pen name "Mark Twain" while working for the *Territorial Enterprise*. Dan De Quille and Mark Twain worked together on the paper, covering all sorts of local happenings. Once they both reviewed a racy melodrama called *Mazeppa* when it came to town. The play starred the voluptuous Adah Isaacs Menken who appeared on stage in flesh-colored tights, tied to the back of a horse! After the show, Adah invited Dan De Quille and Mark Twain up to her hotel room where the two reviewers became involved in a tussle with the actress's pet poodle. Eventually she threw both of her late-night guests out on the street. Dan De Quille's review of her performance was not very enthusiastic. A fellow reporter later commented, "I guess old Dan has discovered that she wears drawers."

Dan De Quille loved to hoodwink his readers into believing that his made-up stories were true. He often would fill his stories with all sorts of "scientific" details. There was the time he reported on the invention of something called "solar armor," an outfit that allegedly would protect the wearer from the intense heat of the Nevada deserts. The armor consisted of a long, loose-fitting jacket and hood made of sponge rubber, connected by a rubber tube to a water-filled pouch. The wearer could squeeze the pouch and send water throughout the suit. As the water evaporated, the temperature of the air near the body would be lowered. Dan reported that a sci-

entist took the solar armor out for a test run in the desert. Unfortunately, he never returned, and his companions later found him frozen stiff. Even though it was over one hundred degrees in the shade, the poor fellow's beard was covered with frost and an icicle hung from his nose. Alas, the solar armor had worked all too well!

Dan de Quille's solar armor story was reprinted in newspapers around the world, and many people believed it to be true. A month after the story appeared in the *Enterprise*, the scientific writer of the *London Times* cited it and suggested that such armor be adopted by the British government in India. In response, Dan sent the *Times* a copy of his article along with a blue-pencil sketch of a western journalist defiantly thumbing his nose. Gotcha that time, crowed a triumphant Dan De Quille.

> **𝔢𝔰 Something More** ... *Visit the colorful offices of the Territorial Enterprise, 53 South C Street, Virginia City, Nevada 89440. Admission is adults $1.00, children $.50. Hours are 10:00 A.M. to 6:00 P.M. daily (winter hours vary). Telephone (702) 847-0525. Read about this pioneer journalist in Richard A. Dwyer and Richard E. Lingenfelter,* Dan De Quille: The Washoe Giant *(1990).*

TALES OF OLD MARIN

The place names along Highway 101 north of San Francisco memorialize California's colorful, multiethnic history. Within the space of a few miles are reminders of Hispanic lumberjacks, English whalers, and fugitive mission Indians.

The town of Corte Madera was once the site of a thriving lumber mill in the days when California was a remote province of the Republic of Mexico. *Corte* is Spanish for cut, and *madera* means timber or lumber. Spanish-speaking lumberjacks worked in the area for years, felling the huge coast redwoods that once covered the surrounding hills. Anglo-American settlers later continued the lumber business and set up their own mill in (where else?) nearby Mill Valley.

Another Spanish place name in southern Marin County is Sausalito, meaning little grove of willows. Sausalito Cove was a favorite anchorage for whalers in the early nineteenth century. Surprising as it sounds today, whaling was once a leading industry in California. Hundreds of whalers from England and the United States sailed to California to hunt gray and humpback whales as they migrated along the coast.

Probably the best known of these early California whalers was an Englishman named William Richardson. He arrived in California in 1822 and promptly fell in love with Doña María Martínez, the daughter of the *comandante* of the San Francisco Presidio. (Foreigners falling in love with a *comandante's* daughter must have been an early San Francisco tradition. Remember Count Rezanov?) After marrying Doña Maria, Richardson stayed in San Francisco and is credited with building the first non-Indian residence within the present city limits. His adobe house stood on what is now Grant Avenue between Clay and Washington streets. Richardson also owned an enormous rancho in Marin, bordering the bay that today bears his name.

In the early 1820s, a California Indian escaped from Mission Dolores in San Francisco and fled to Marin. The Indian had been baptized at the mission and given the Christian name Quintin, but apparently he decided to return to his old ways. As Quintin surely must have known, leaving the mission without permission was strictly forbidden. Soldiers were dispatched to bring him back. Eventually the soldiers recaptured him on the point in Marin County now called Point San Quentin. There are a couple of ironies here. American mapmakers, ignorant of the story of Quintin, later added a "San" or "Saint" in front of his name, hardly appropriate for a man who had fled from those who had sought to convert him. Still later, Point San Quentin became the site of the state's first maximum security prison. Another ironic tribute to a man who was himself a fugitive!

> *Something More* ... *View the commemorative plaque that marks the site of William Richardson's home at 815–829 Grant Avenue in San Francisco. Also visit the San Quentin State Prison Museum (opening in January 1992), Building #106, Dolores Way, San Quentin 94964. Telephone (415) 454-1460 for museum hours and admission fees. A good book on Marin County's history is Jack Mason,* Early Marin *(1971). Another useful reference book is Erwin G. Gudde,* California Place Names *(1969).*

MURALS OF COIT TOWER

Perhaps the most identifiable landmark of the San Francisco skyline is Coit Tower, that concrete obelisk perched in splendid isolation atop Telegraph Hill. Inside the tower is a fascinating panorama of California cultural history, the Coit Tower Murals.

Painted during a six-month period in the depths of the Great Depression, the murals seemed to offer something for everyone. Sports fans could enjoy *Collegiate Sports*, a mural of the Cal Berkeley–Stanford Big Game. Journalists could relate to *Newsgathering*, a panel depicting reporters and editors frantically trying to beat a deadline. There's even a mural for survivors of the stock market crash of 1929. *Stockbroker* shows a denizen of Montgomery Street standing confidently amid reams of ticker tape with a phone grasped firmly in one hand. My favorite mural is *San Francisco Bay*, a dreamy portrait of the bay in the 1930s, crisscrossed by gleaming white ferries steaming off in all directions.

The murals were commissioned in 1933 by the Public Works of Art Project (PWAP), one of the many "alphabet soup" agencies of the New Deal created to provide jobs for the unemployed. (Remember the WPA, the PWA, and the CCC?) Initial plans for the interior of Coit Tower had been to use it as a museum for pioneer memorabilia, but the PWAP decided instead that it would be a likely place to put unemployed California artists to work. The federal government hired more than two dozen artists to cover the walls with murals and paid them an average wage of $31.22 a week.

The paintings stirred up quite a controversy. Some included left-wing images such as a newsstand copy of *The Daily Worker*, Karl Marx's *Das Kapital* on a library shelf, and the dreaded symbol of the Soviet Union, a hammer and sickle. When news leaked out what the artists were up to, some folks strongly objected. Conservatives argued that this kind of art should not be supported by public funds. Right-wing vigilantes threatened to storm the tower and chisel out the offending murals! Fortunately the murals were not destroyed, and the tower opened to the public without incident on October 20, 1934.

One local critic viewed the controversy with bemused detachment:

> There is something about [art] when it is applied to the walls of public buildings that seems to breed dissension. There have always been naughty little boys who drew vilifications on schoolroom walls when their teachers were not looking. Likewise, there have always been mischievous little artists who put something over while they were not being watched. Of such substance is history made.

ॐ *Something More* ... *See the murals for yourself by visiting Coit Tower, Telegraph Hill, San Francisco 94133. Admission is adults $3.00, seniors $2.00, and children $1.00. Hours are 10:00 A.M. to 5:00 P.M. daily. Telephone (415) 274-0203. Elevator rides to the top are a must! The best guide to the murals and their history is Masha Zakheim Jewett,* Coit Tower, San Francisco: Its History and Art *(1983).*

HORROR AND HEROISM
IN THE HIGH SIERRA

The tragic story of the Donner party is familiar to many Californians, but few realize how the Donners got stuck in the Sierra Nevada in the first place. Probably the biggest problem for the Donner party was the bad advice they received from a guidebook, *The Emigrants' Guide to Oregon and California* (by Lanford W. Hastings, 1845), which suggested that travelers to California take a shortcut south of the Great Salt Lake. It turned out that the shortcut was really a long-cut, and it cost the Donners about one month extra travel time. *The Emigrants' Guide* was just one of many worthless guidebooks churned out for unsuspecting western travelers in the 1840s and 1850s. (Another popular

guide was published by D. L. Snyder. On the title page of a surviving copy, some disillusioned purchaser speculated that the author's initials, D. L., probably stood for "Damn Liar.") At any rate, the Donner party's delay in reaching the Sierra meant that the group would be entering the mountains dangerously late in the year.

The Donner party began their ascent of the Sierra in October 1846 and had the misfortune of being caught near the summit during the heaviest snowfall in thirty years. The snow reached an incredible depth of twenty-two feet! The tall stone monument at Donner State Park near Truckee marks the snow level when the Donner party was there. During that terrible winter, the group lived in crude log cabins and lean-tos they put together with great difficulty. When food provisions ran out, first the pack animals were eaten, then the hides and the boiled leather from snowshoes, and finally the flesh of those who died. Only about half of the eighty-seven members of the party survived the winter.

Four different rescue parties braved the dangers of the high Sierra to bring out the survivors. Some of the would-be rescuers became victims themselves, dying among the drifts of snow. The rescuers of the Donner party have been justly praised as great heroes in California history, but they also were quite human. A fellow named Sept Moultry petitioned Congress for an honorarium of twenty thousand dollars for his heroism, while others were a bit more modest. Ned Coffeemeyer, for instance, itemized his "rescue expenses" as one flannel shirt, a pair of stockings, and one pair of store-bought drawers. Even in the midst of great tragedy and heroism, I guess it's still important to keep track of those expenses!

> ₹● **Something More** … *Have a picnic at the Donner Monument and tour the Visitors Center at Donner State Park, Donner Lake 95737. Follow signs to the state park from Interstate 80. Admission to the Visitors Center is adults $2.00 and children $1.00. Hours are 10:00 A.M. to 12:00 P.M., and 1:00 P.M. to 4:00 P.M. daily. Telephone (916) 587-3841. The classic account of the Donner party tragedy is George R. Stewart,* Ordeal by Hunger *(1936).*

THE BIG FOUR
UNDER ATTACK

ew names in California history are more familiar than those of Leland Stanford, Collis P. Huntington, Charles Crocker, and Mark Hopkins. Known collectively as the Big Four, these worthy gentlemen started out by building and running the Central Pacific and Southern Pacific railroads. Eventually they controlled a virtual monopoly on transportation in California and exercised enormous political power. Quite simply, they were the richest and most powerful Californians of their era.

What is perhaps not so well known is that the Big Four were under almost constant attack. Many of their fellow Californians came to believe that these four railroad tycoons had amassed too much wealth and power. They charged that the Big Four's transportation monopoly was draining the profit from every other business enterprise in the state and that their political machine was corrupting California government.

Anger against the Big Four was graphically expressed in contemporary editorials and political cartoons. In 1882, the *San Francisco Wasp* published "The Curse of California," a cartoon comparing the Big Four to a giant octopus. The eyes of this grotesque monster were the heads of Stanford and Crocker, and in its outstretched tentacles lay the limp forms of California farmers, fruit growers, miners, and shippers. The message of the cartoon was clear: The wealth of California was being misdirected into the bloated money bags of the Big Four in their mansions atop Nob Hill.

One of the most devastating anti-Big Four cartoons appeared in the *San Francisco Examiner* in 1898. "Highwayman Huntington to the Voters of California" pictured the president of the Southern Pacific Railroad as a vicious gunman, complete with skull cufflinks and a garish diamond stickpin. Holding a gun aimed directly at the voters of California, this ruffian commanded, "Hand Over Your Honor, Manhood, and Independence, and Be Quick About It!" Huntington was not amused.

HIGHWAYMAN HUNTINGTON TO THE VOTERS OF CALIFORNIA:

"Hand Over Your Honor, Manhood and Independence, and Be Quick About It."

The following year, several bills aimed at silencing offending journalists were introduced in the railroad-dominated state legislature. One proposal made it easier to prosecute a newspaper for libel. Another declared that the killing of a newspaperman who libeled a citizen was justifiable homicide. (Fortunately this did not pass.) Another bill effectively banned the future publication of political cartoons in the state. It prohibited the publishing of any cartoon which reflected adversely upon the "honor, integrity, manhood, virtue, or reputation" of any individual. This anti-cartoon bill became law in

1899 and remained on the books for over fifteen years, a chilling legacy from the era of the Big Four.

ها *Something More* ... *View the display of Big Four political cartoons at the California State Railroad Museum at the corner of Second and "I" streets, Old Sacramento 95814. Admission is adults $5.00 and children $2.00. Hours are 10:00 A.M. to 5:00 P.M. daily. Telephone (916) 448-4466. See also the excellent collection in Ed Salzman and Anne Leigh Brown,* The Cartoon History of California Politics *(1978).*

WHEN HOLLYWOOD
WAS IN THE EAST BAY

ention the word "Hollywood" to a movie fan any-
where in the world and you're likely to conjure up
images of glamour and romance. Now try the word
"Niles" and see what you get—probably nothing more
than an uncomprehending, blank stare. Such are the vagaries of history, for it was Niles, not Hollywood, that once seemed destined to
be the home of the California film industry.

The first major motion picture to be produced in the United
States was filmed in the New Jersey countryside in 1903. *The Great
Train Robbery* was an eight-minute, one-reel western, produced by
the film company of Thomas Edison and starring an ex-vaudevillian
named Gilbert Anderson as Bronco Billy. At the time, Edison and a
few others controlled the patents on nearly all the available motion-
picture cameras and projectors. Independent or "outlaw" filmmakers
soon rebelled against Edison's monopoly. One of these indepen-
dents was none other than ol' Bronco Billy himself, Gilbert Anderson. In 1908, Anderson began scouting the country for a location to
launch his own film company; he wanted to be as far away as possible from Edison's patent attorneys. Eventually he found an ideal
location southeast of Oakland in a rugged little canyon near the East
Bay village of Niles.

Given Gilbert Anderson's success with his career-launching
film, it's not surprising that he specialized in producing westerns.
What is rather amazing is the *number* of westerns he produced.
Beginning in 1908 and continuing for the next six years, Anderson
and his crew ground out some 375 films in Niles Canyon—more
than one a week! They all starred, of course, that lovable cowpoke
Bronco Billy.

Other stars also made their way to Niles Canyon. Ben Turpin,
Wallace Beery, William S. Hart, and "America's Sweetheart," Mary
Pickford, all played in films shot in Niles. Mary Pickford starred in
one of Anderson's most successful productions, *Rebecca of Sunny-*

Hendrick

brook Farm. Probably the best known actor to work in Niles Canyon was Charlie Chaplin, lured there by Anderson's offer of a contract paying $1,250 per week (nearly ten times what Chaplin had been making at rival Keystone Films). Chaplin finished five pictures at Niles, including *The Tramp* in which he perfected his trademark costume of bowler hat, pinched black suit, and oversized shoes.

Eventually the motion picture industry abandoned Niles Canyon for Southern California. Hollywood offered a superior climate, a greater variety of landscapes, and something that Northern California simply couldn't match—easy access to the Mexican border across which worried filmmakers could flee to escape those pesky patent attorneys from New Jersey!

> 🐦 *Something More* ... *Visit the town of Niles and see the few remaining buildings left from the days when "Hollywood was in the East Bay." Find your way to the corner of Niles Boulevard and "H" Street. The two-story structure on the east side of "H" Street was the original Wesley Hotel where Charlie Chaplin stayed. Walk south one block to Second Street and turn right, pass "G" Street, and on the right (from 37268 to 37374 Second Street) you'll see a row of small, doll-like homes built around 1910 for the actors. A comprehensive guide to the early California film industry is Terry Ramsaye,* A Million and One Nights *(1986).*

The Wickedest Man in San Francisco

mbrose Gwinnett Bierce, known to his detractors as "Almighty God Bierce" and "Bitter Bierce," was the author of what was once the most widely read and most widely feared newspaper column in San Francisco. Bierce worked for William Randolph Hearst at the *San Francisco Examiner*, and in his daily columns he mercilessly attacked his victims. He once denounced M. H. de Young of the rival *San Francisco Chronicle* as "a liar and a scoundrel" and "a chimpanzee." In another column, he took on a corrupt state senator. "The very fat on his entrails," thundered Bierce, "belongs to the widows and orphans he has robbed." Bierce even attacked man's best friend, claiming that dogs were nothing more than "smilers and defilers, reekers and leakers."

Bierce was a prolific writer. He produced several novels and many macabre short stories, some of which were real spine-tinglers. Probably his most popular book was *The Devil's Dictionary* (1906), a collection of exceedingly bitter and pessimistic definitions of common words. For example:

> *History*, n., An account, mostly false, of events mostly unimportant, which are brought about by rulers mostly knaves, and soldiers mostly fools.

> *Litigation*, n., A machine which you go into as a pig and come out as a sausage.

> *Love*, n., A temporary insanity, curable by marriage.

> *Quill*, n., An implement of torture yielded by a goose and commonly wielded by an ass.

> *Saint*, n., A dead sinner, revised and edited.

Bierce eventually resigned from the *Examiner* and went into semiretirement. He then had the crazy idea of going to Mexico during the Pancho Villa revolution. He headed south across the border in 1913, never to return. No one knows for sure just what happened to old Ambrose Bierce, but one of his last letters gives us a tantalizing clue to his fate:

> If you should hear of my being stood up against a Mexican stone wall and shot to rags please know that I think it is a pretty good way to depart this life. It beats old age, disease or falling down the cellar stairs. To be a *gringo* in Mexico—ah, that is euthanasia!

🙐 ***Something More*** *... Read about Ambrose Bierce in either Paul Fatout,* Ambrose Bierce, the Devil's Lexicographer *(1951) or Richard Saunders,* Ambrose Bierce: The Making of a Misanthrope *(1984). The enigmatic story of Bierce was also the inspiration for Carlos Fuentes,* Old Gringo *(1985), later made into a film of the same name starring Gregory Peck and Jane Fonda.*

THE MINER'S
TEN COMMANDMENTS

One of the great joys of traveling to faraway places is sending picture postcards to the folks back home. During the California gold rush, one of the most sought-after items was a type of souvenir stationery known as a "letter sheet." Illustrated with text or engravings of California scenes, the letter sheets could be folded to form self-made envelopes.

The most popular of the letter sheets was called "The Miner's Ten Commandments." The First Commandment was simple and direct: "Thou shalt have no other claim than one."

The Sixth Commandment was a bit more complex, but just as important:

> Thou shalt not kill thy body by working in the rain.... Neither shalt thou kill thy neighbor's body in a duel.... Neither shalt thou destroy thyself by getting "tight," nor "stewed," nor "high," nor "corned," nor "three sheets in the wind," by drinking smoothly down "brandy slings," "gin cock-tails," "whisky punches," nor "egg nogs." Neither shalt thou suck through a straw...nor gurgle from a bottle the raw material.

The Eighth Commandment had to have been the toughest:

> Thou shalt not steal a pick, or a pan, or a shovel, from thy fellow miner, nor take away his tools without his leave...for he will be sure to discover what thou hast done, and will straightway call his fellow miners together, and if the law hinder them not they will hang thee, or give thee fifty lashes, or shave thy head and brand thee like a horse thief with "R" upon thy cheek.

The Tenth Commandment offered tender advice for men everywhere who find themselves far from home:

Thou shalt not commit unsuitable matrimony, nor covet "single
blessedness," nor forget absent maidens, nor neglect thy first love;
but thou shalt consider how faithfully and patiently she waiteth thy
return; yea, and covereth each epistle that thou sendeth with kisses
of kindly welcome until she hath thyself.

"The Miner's Ten Commandments" was created by an
English-born author and editor named James Mason Hutchings.
Hutchings came to California in 1849 to try his hand at mining, but
soon found he could make far more money with his pen than his
pick. His famous letter sheet of 1853 sold over one hundred thousand copies in its first year, and from its profits he founded

Hutchings' California Magazine in 1858. Hutchings later was able to retire to Yosemite where he opened the valley's first hotel and enjoyed for years a near monopoly on the tourist trade. Whether he kept his guests well supplied with postcards or letter sheets is not recorded.

> 🐛 ***Something More*** ... *View the collection of California letter sheets in the California State Library, Library Courts Building, 914 Capitol Mall, Room 304, between 9th, 10th, and "N" streets in Sacramento 94237. Free. Hours are 8:00 A.M. to 5:00 P.M. Monday through Friday. Telephone (916) 445-4149. Visit the grave of James Mason Hutchings as well as other famous California pioneers in the Yosemite National Park Cemetery, located on the valley floor adjacent to the Visitors Center. Telephone (209) 372-0299.*

THE VANISHING EVANGELIST

imee Semple McPherson is one of the most fascinating women in California history. Known to the faithful as Sister Aimee, she was an itinerant evangelist who arrived in Los Angeles in 1918 with her mother, two children, and, as she liked to say, "a hundred dollars and a tambourine." She was recently divorced, having been married twice to men in the ministry.

In Los Angeles, Sister Aimee really hit the big time. She built a huge five-thousand-seat temple for her Church of the Four Square Gospel and started America's first religious radio station, KFSG. (The station ran afoul of the Federal Communications Commission when it was discovered that the KFSG transmitter was so powerful it interfered with the signals of other local stations.) Someone once called Sister Aimee the "Mary Pickford of Revivalism." Perhaps she did look more like a starlet than a preacher. She was a slender, attractive blond who enjoyed wearing elaborate costumes and staging vaudeville-style religious services. She once startled her congregation on a Sunday morning by riding into the pulpit on a motorcycle! But for all her flash and pizzazz, Sister Aimee had a serious side. She and her congregation ministered to the sick, the hungry, and the homeless of Los Angeles.

One afternoon in the spring of 1926, Sister Aimee went for a swim in the ocean and never returned. Her distraught followers waited and prayed for three days while the police led a massive search off the coast for Sister Aimee. Finally, her grieving mother declared Sister Aimee dead by drowning and held a memorial service at the temple. Then, in what seemed like a miraculous return from the dead, Sister Aimee reappeared. She told police she had been kidnapped and held in Mexico by two men and a woman who wanted her to heal their sick child. She then escaped and wandered in the desert until she found help.

Sister Aimee's homecoming in Los Angeles was a spectacular affair. The police escorted her from the train, thousands of people lined the streets, and an airplane showered rose petals in her path.

She returned triumphant to the pulpit and told her followers the dramatic story of her kidnapping and harrowing escape.

Ah, but there was trouble in Southern California when some investigative reporters began snooping around. They uncovered evidence that the kidnapping story was a hoax. The truth was Sister Aimee had spent her disappearance in a cottage in Carmel, enjoying what the reporters called an "illicit vacation" in the company of the engineer from her radio station!

> 🕿 ***Something More*** ... *Visit Sister Aimee's Angelus Temple at 1100 Glendale Boulevard, Los Angeles 90026. Free. Telephone (213) 484-1100. Hours are 9:00 A.M. to 5:00 P.M. Monday through Friday. Call in advance for a special tour. Her pulpit and other memorabilia are on display in the History Gallery at the Oakland Museum, 1000 Oak Street, corner of Tenth and Oak, Oakland 94607. Free. Hours are 10:00 A.M. to 5:00 P.M. Wednesday through Saturday, and 12:00 P.M. to 7:00 P.M. Sunday. Telephone (415) 273-3401. A good biography of Sister Aimee is Lately Thomas,* The Vanishing Evangelist *(1959).*

A PRESIDIO LOVE STORY

ack when the San Francisco Presidio was a lonely out-post of the Spanish empire, it became the setting for a tragic love affair between Doña Concepción Argüello, the beautiful fifteen-year-old daughter of the Spanish *comandante*, and Count Nikolai Rezanov, the forty-two-year-old commander of the Russian brig *Juno*.

Count Rezánov sailed into San Francisco Bay in 1806, hoping to establish trade relations with the Spanish. Shortly after his arrival, Doña Concepción entered his life and his social calendar. Whether the Count was motivated primarily by romance or by economics we can never be sure, but we do know he and the vivacious young San Franciscan soon became engaged.

Perhaps it was over a supper of quesadillas and borscht when the happy couple broke the news to Doña Concepción's parents who were understandably shocked at the engagement. First, there was the matter of religion. Rezánov was Eastern Orthodox; the Argüellos were Roman Catholic. Then there was the difference in their ages, an awesome twenty-seven years! Finally, after some parental dithering and handwringing, the Argüellos agreed to the engagement on the condition that an appeal first be made to Rome for permission.

Meanwhile, Count Rezánov was summoned back to Russia. At their parting, the two lovers pledged their undying devotion to one another. Doña Concepción placed around the Count's neck a small gold locket containing two strands of hair—hers intertwined with his. The Count then sailed away, never to return. While cross-ing Siberia on horseback, he was thrown from his horse and fatally injured. As he lay dying, Rezánov asked a soldier to promise to find Doña Concepción, tell her of his love, and return to her the locket. It was five years before a messenger reached California and delivered to Doña Concepción the sad news along with the locket. She was devastated.

Bret Harte later wrote a romantic poem about Doña Concepción in which he claimed that she spent the next fifty years

as a trembling, wasted figure, in perpetual mourning for her lost Russian lover. In reality, she led a long and full life, devoting herself to caring for the homeless and hungry, becoming something of an early-day Mother Teresa. Known as *La Beata*, "the Blessed One," those who knew Doña Concepción in her latter days said she was a jolly old soul, spreading laughter and good cheer wherever she went.

> ❧ *Something More* ... *Visit the grave of Doña Concepción in St. Dominic's Cemetery, corner of Hillcrest Avenue and East 5th Street, Benicia 94510. Free. Open daylight hours daily. Bret Harte's poem can be found in his book,* Complete Poetical Works *(1902). Another version of this romantic tale appears in Gertrude Atherton,* My San Francisco: A Wayward Biography *(1946).*

THE MISSED CUE
OF COMMODORE JONES

One of the strangest episodes in California history is the premature invasion of Monterey by a squad of United States Marines in 1842. California was then a part of Mexico, and this embarrassing gaffe put quite a strain on relations between the United States and Mexico.

It all started when Commodore Thomas ap Catesby Jones, an impetuous young naval officer, got wind of a rumor that the United States and Mexico were at war. Commodore Jones was under standing orders that, in the event of such a war, he was to set sail and seize Monterey, the capital of Mexican California.

On October 18, Jones sailed confidently into Monterey Bay. The next day he sent a delegation ashore to demand that the Mexican officials surrender by nine o'clock the following morning. Needless to say, the Mexican officials were rather startled and confused by Jones's demand—they had heard nothing of any war. They stayed up half the night debating whether to fight or surrender. Around midnight they finally decided to give up.

The next morning, a triumphant Jones landed 150 marines and sailors on the beach at Monterey in time to witness the Mexican troops marching out of the Presidio to surrender "with music and colors flying." The marines lowered the Mexican flag, raised the Stars and Stripes, fired a salute, and proclaimed California under the benevolent control of the United States of America.

Unfortunately Commodore Jones had made a big mistake! He soon learned that the rumor about war was false. With all the dignity he could muster, Jones apologized to the Mexican authorities, lowered the United States flag, raised the Mexican flag again, and fired another salute. He hustled his marines back on board ship, and sailed off into the sunset. An unhappy Mexican government lodged a strong protest in Washington, demanding that Jones be severely reprimanded. Instead, Jones was given a mild slap on the wrist.

It was just four years later that the marines once again invaded the California coast. However, this time it was for real, and the conquest was permanent. I think of Commodore Jones as an unfortunate actor on that great stage of history who happened to miss his cue. He came bounding out on stage just a moment too soon and, in great embarrassment, was hooked off into the wings. Timing, I guess, is everything.

🐾 *Something More* ... *Visit the Presidio of Monterey Museum, located on Private Ewing Road, inside the presidio gates, Monterey 93944. Free. Hours are 1:00 P.M. to 4:00 P.M. Monday through Friday, and 10:00 A.M. to 4:00 P.M. Saturday. Telephone (408) 647-5414. The complete story is told in George B. Brooke, "The Vest Pocket War of Commodore Jones,"* Pacific Historical Review *(August 1962).*

LONG DAY'S JOURNEY INTO...DANVILLE

Probably few Bay Area residents are aware that one of America's greatest playwrights, Eugene O'Neill, once lived in the hills above Danville. O'Neill was a brooding soul, the product of a tragic and unhappy childhood. His father was an itinerant actor, his mother a drug addict, and his brother died of alcoholism. In his early twenties, Eugene was stricken by tuberculosis and attempted suicide. Yet out of these tragic circumstances came some of the most enduring plays ever written by an American. Eugene O'Neill won four Pulitzer Prizes and remains today the only American playwright ever to win the Nobel Prize for literature.

Eugene O'Neill moved to California in 1936, seeking solitude and privacy for his writing. At first he thought he'd settle on some land in Marin County's Lucas Valley, but decided instead on property in the San Ramon Valley of Contra Costa County. He used the forty thousand dollars from his Nobel Prize to buy fifteen acres in the hills above Danville. There he built his home, Tao (pronounced "dow") House. He lived there with his wife Carlotta and daughter Oona until 1944. During that time, eighteen-year-old Oona married the fifty-four-year-old movie star Charlie Chaplin. The marriage so outraged O'Neill he severed all relations with his daughter.

In his study overlooking the San Ramon Valley, Eugene O'Neill wrote such classics as *The Ice Man Cometh* and *Long Day's Journey Into Night*. But life wasn't all work and no play at Tao House. O'Neill indulged in a couple of favorite amusements while living there. He enjoyed especially "Rosie," his antique player piano decorated with fanciful drawings of naked ladies. He would drop in a few nickels and enjoy listening to ragtime tunes or singing along with visiting buddies like folk singer Burl Ives and publisher Bennett Cerf.

O'Neill's pet dalmatian, Silverdene Emblem O'Neill, better known as Blemie, was not only a source of amusement but a close

companion as well. Blemie and his master would take off for long walks in the surrounding East Bay hills, and the dalmatian would run and play to his heart's content. When Blemie died in December 1940, both Eugene and Carlotta were bereft. To mark the occasion, O'Neill composed Blemie's "Last Will and Testament." The departed dalmatian left these words of comfort for his grieving master and mistress:

Whenever you visit my grave, say to yourselves with regret but also with happiness in your hearts at the remembrance of my long happy life with you: "Here lies one who loved us and whom we loved." No matter how deep my sleep I shall hear you, and not all the power of death can keep my spirit from wagging a grateful tail.

Something More ... *Visit Tao House (and Blemie's grave), now a part of the Eugene O'Neill National Historic Site. Reservations are required. Telephone (415) 838-0249. There is a mandatory shuttle bus ride from downtown Danville up to the house. The guided tour is free and available Wednesday through Sunday by the National Park Service. The full story is available in Arthur Gelb's biography,* O'Neill *(1974).*

FROM GRIZZLY BEAR
TO NATIONAL PARK

The origin of the name "Yosemite" is a matter of some controversy, but the name probably comes from a Miwok Indian word meaning grizzly bear. The Miwok had lived in the area for thousands of years and had developed a healthy respect for the power of the grizzly. The Miwok word for the valley was *A-wa-ni*, from which we get the name for the Ahwahnee Hotel built in the early 1920s.

The first Anglo-Americans to see Yosemite Valley were a party of beaver trappers who stumbled upon it in 1833. The next recorded sighting came eighteen years later when a band of state militia invaded the valley in pursuit of "hostiles." The militiamen were led by the Blond King of the Tulare, a veteran Indian fighter named James D. Savage. Savage is credited with giving the valley its present name. Tourists first visited Yosemite in 1855, brought in by James Mason Hutchings, an Englishman who had made a small fortune publishing "The Miners Ten Commandments." Hutchings settled in the valley in 1860, built a hotel, and for many years profitably cultivated the Yosemite tourist trade.

Much of the credit for the creation of Yosemite National Park properly belongs to the Scottish-born naturalist John Muir. Muir first visited Yosemite Valley in 1868, and like so many visitors before and since he was immediately struck by the beauty of the towering granite walls. The scene was "incomparable," Muir wrote, "like an immense hall or temple lighted from above." He built himself a little cabin, with ferns growing inside, on the valley floor. It was, he said, "a little bit of paradise."

Over the years, John Muir grew more and more disturbed by the commercial development of Yosemite. Loggers, sheep ranchers, and tourists were taking their toll on its natural beauty. Determined to protect Yosemite, Muir began a vigorous lobbying campaign for the creation of a national park. At last, in the fall of 1890, Congress passed a bill creating Yosemite National Park. The original park, however, included only the land surrounding the valley. It wasn't until 1906 that federal protection was extended to the valley as well.

Today Yosemite National Park is a monument to one of the great victories of the conservation movement. With more than three million visitors a year, it also stands as a challenge to all those who share John Muir's conviction that the preservation of nature's beauty is a sacred trust of each generation.

> 🐾 *Something More* ... *Tour the Visitors Center, Yosemite National Park, P. O. Box 577, Yosemite 95389. Telephone (209) 372-0299. Summer hours are 8:00 A.M. to 8:00 P.M. Winter hours are 9:00 A.M. to 5:00 P.M. There is no fee to enter the Visitors Center, but the entry fee to the park is $5.00 per vehicle. Several new histories of the park were published to mark its centennial in 1990. Among the best are Alfred Runte,* Yosemite: The Embattled Wilderness *(1990) and Shirley Sargent,* Yosemite, the First 100 Years *(1988).*

TELEGRAPH HILL

ave you ever noticed that the sides of San Francisco's Telegraph Hill look as though they'd been gnawed by some giant rock-eating monster? Actually those huge patches of bare earth and rock are scars left behind from years of rock quarrying. From about 1860 until the late 1890s, mining companies relentlessly blasted away at the hill, dislodging rocks and gravel for construction projects all around the city.

Needless to say, all that blasting and digging were a real nuisance for the folks who lived on Telegraph Hill. Not only were the noise and dust terrific, but frequent landslides posed a constant danger to life and property. Several homes actually slid down the hill because their foundations had been blown away. Residents became so angry they began stoning the quarry workers—and they had plenty of projectiles to choose from! At last, in the 1890s, the residents of the hill won an injunction to halt the quarrying operations.

One of California's first telegraph lines was installed on the hill in 1853. The line carried messages from Point Lobos, near Seal Rocks. Before the electric telegraph, merchants had built an observation station on the hill and topped it with a tall black pole and a semaphore. (A semaphore is a kind of signaling device with two long arms.) When a horseback rider posted near the Golden Gate sighted a ship heading toward the bay, he would alert the semaphore operator atop Telegraph Hill. The operator would then position the semaphore arms to signal the kind of ship arriving. One position of the arms signaled a schooner, for instance, while another position meant a steamship or side-wheeler. When the town merchants saw the semaphore being positioned, they would rush to the Embarcadero to get first crack at whatever valuable cargo the ship was bringing to port.

The merchants were not the only San Franciscans who understood the semaphore signals. Nearly everyone did. One night at a theater in the city, an actor stepped up to the footlights, extended both his arms in a dramatic gesture, and cried out, "What does this mean?" From somewhere in the darkened audience came the enthusiastic reply, "A side-wheel steamer!"

> 🕿 *Something More* ... *Visit the base of Telegraph Hill at the intersection of Montgomery and Lombard streets in San Francisco to view the ravaged sides of the hill. The story is well told in David F. Myrick,* San Francisco's Telegraph Hill *(1972) and Doris Muscatine,* Old San Francisco: The Biography of a City from Early Days to the Earthquake *(1975).*

California's Roving Capital

Did you know that the state capital hasn't always been Sacramento? For years the capital moved around so often one pundit suggested the whole thing should be put on wheels!

The problem began when the early lawmakers failed to designate a permanent state capital. In a remarkable display of fiscal responsibility, they left its location open to future bids from rival towns. They hoped thereby to acquire land and buildings for the capital without cost to the state government.

San Jose was the first city to enter the capital sweepstakes. The state legislature assembled there for its first session on December 15, 1849. The proceedings were not altogether as stately as one might have hoped. Contemporary critics dubbed it "the legislature of a thousand drinks," but that's another story.

Over the next five years, the capital was hawked about in a most undignified manner. In June 1851, the legislators moved to Vallejo, but were then lured back to San Jose, back to Vallejo, to Sacramento, back to Vallejo again, and then to Benicia. There the legislators took a breather, enjoying for several months the splendid accommodations at the new Benicia City Hall. But even this was not to be their final resting spot. At last, in 1854, the legislators settled on Sacramento as their permanent headquarters. The legislature met in the Sacramento County Courthouse until construction of the present state capitol was completed in 1869.

More than a century later, in the early 1970s, the legislature launched a massive architectural restoration campaign to bring the capitol up to seismic safety standards and to restore it to its turn-of-the-century grandeur. One of the conundrums of the restoration project was the proper color for the restored capitol dome. The original copper dome had been expected to weather to a beautiful verdigris green, but that never happened. Over the years it turned, instead, to a rather nondescript muddy brown. Later the dome was painted green, then gold, and eventually white.

A high-ranking state legislator, noted for his wit if not his veracity, once told me the architects resolved this great issue by deciding to cover the restored dome with copper and to hasten its proper weathering by treating it with a mixture of vinegar and urine. My legislative informant heartily approved of this resolution. "If there's one thing my colleagues here in Sacramento need," he said with a wink and a nod, "it's a little more piss and vinegar!"

&♥ *Something More* ... *Visit the California State Capitol Museum, Room B-27, State Capitol, Sacramento 95814, located between L and N streets on Tenth Street. Free. Hours are 9:00 A.M. to 5:00 P.M. daily. Tours of several restored "period" rooms available. Telephone (916) 324-0333. The complete restoration story can be found in Lynn Marlowe,* California State Capital: A Pictorial History *(1983). The history of California's capitol is also told in Henry-Russell Hitchcock and William Seale,* Temples of Democracy *(1976).*

SAINTS, CATS, AND TRUNKS OF THE SOUTH BAY

an Francisco South Bay commuters are all too familiar with the dreaded litany: "There's a jack-knifed big rig on the Guadalupe Parkway, an overturned vehicle on Stevens Creek Boulevard, and fender benders on the streets of Los Gatos and Saratoga." When you are already immobilized in bumper-to-bumper traffic, these words can cause even the most seasoned commuter to pound the steering wheel in agonizing frustration.

One way to relieve the stress of the daily commute is to reflect on the colorful history of the places now snarled with traffic. Take Guadalupe Parkway, for instance. This story goes all the way back to one of the most revered moments in Mexican history, the appearance of the Virgin Mary to a poor peasant named Juan Diego on a hill outside Mexico City in the sixteenth century. This miraculous vision became known as the Virgin of Guadalupe and she eventually was adopted as the patron saint of Mexico. When Spanish-speaking pioneers passed through the South Bay in 1776, it was only natural for them to name its principal river the *Rio de Nuestra Señora de Guadalupe* (the River of Our Lady of Guadalupe). The river later gave its name to the parkway.

The story of nearby Stevens Creek Boulevard reminds us that English-speaking pioneers began arriving overland in the early 1840s. Stevens Creek was named for Captain Elisha Stevens, an American trapper and frontiersman who led the first wagon train over the Sierra Nevada in 1844. Stevens discovered what was later called Donner Pass. Like the Donner party, the Stevens party was caught in an early snowstorm, and some of its members were forced to spend the winter at Donner Lake. Fortunately, unlike the Donner party, the Stevens party survived the ordeal without losing any of its members. Captain Stevens later settled on a ranch along the creek now bearing his name.

Most folks are probably aware that Los Gatos means "the cats" in Spanish. And we're not talking here about little pussycats! The name comes from the rather intimidating wildcats or bobcats that once roamed freely over much of California. They were quite common in the South Bay, so it was natural that one of the early ranchos of the area was named *Rinconada de los Gatos*, or Cats' Corner.

There's a difference of opinion about the origin of the name Saratoga. Some think it comes from the Saratoga trunk, a type of trunk with a rounded top that many of the pioneers brought with them on their way west. More likely, however, the name derives from the nearby mineral springs that reminded early residents of the Saratoga Springs resort in upstate New York. The town was founded in 1851 by an Irish miller named Martin McCarthy, and for twenty years it was known as McCarthysville. Eventually the local residents opted for the more sonorous Saratoga—although I'm not sure that news of a fender "smashed in Saratoga" is any more welcome today than hearing of one "mashed in McCarthysville."

& **Something More** ... *Visit the San Jose Historical Museum at 1600 Senter Road, San Jose 95112. Admission is adults $2.00, seniors $1.50, and children $1.00. Hours are 10:00 A.M. to 4:30 P.M. Monday through Friday and 12:00 P.M. to 4:30 P.M. weekends. Telephone (408) 287-2290.*

THE DROP-OUT WHO DROPPED IN

ere's some comforting news for anxious parents whose college-age sons or daughters have threatened to abandon their studies and leave school before earning their degrees. Three of the great classics in California literature—Richard Henry Dana's *Two Years before the Mast* (1840), Frank Norris's *The Octopus* (1901), and John Steinbeck's *The Grapes of Wrath* (1939)—were all written by college drop-outs.

Richard Henry Dana, member of a blue-blooded New England family, dropped out of Harvard University in 1834 complaining of strained eyesight. Hoping to restore his health, and to escape from the narrow confines of his provincial world, Dana decided to take a job as a common seaman. He signed on board a merchant ship sailing for California in what was called the "hide and tallow trade."

Two Years before the Mast tells the story of Dana's adventures in Mexican California collecting cowhides and large sacks of rendered fat or tallow from the coastal ranchos. These raw materials were gathered for shipment to Boston where they were to be made into such things as saddles, soap, and candles. Dana was given the job of hauling the stiffened cowhides down to the shore, piling them on his head, and then wading out through the surf to load them on board ship. It was nothing like the work he had done at Harvard, he noted, but at least he was still using his head!

Dana was deeply impressed by California. He especially liked the climate, which he believed to be the finest in all the world. He also enjoyed the social life of Mexican California. He described in colorful detail a wedding he attended at a rancho in Santa Barbara. It was quite an affair, he wrote, lasting for three days of partying and dancing the fandango. He was fascinated by the quaint California custom of breaking an eggshell filled with cologne over the head of someone you admired. In May 1836, Dana sailed back to Boston with mixed emotions about leaving this exotic land.

Richard Henry Dana returned to the West Coast more than twenty years later. He was amazed at how completely the thousands of newcomers who had arrived during the California gold rush had changed the state. Dana was also intrigued by how California had transformed those who had settled there. He encountered in San Francisco a man he had known fifteen years earlier in New England. Back home the fellow had been a rather reserved and conservative church deacon, but *now* he was a Californian. "He walked with a stride," Dana observed, "an uplifted countenance, his face covered with beard, whiskers, and mustache, his voice strong and natural— in short, he had put off the New England deacon and become a human being." What a difference California makes!

> 🐌 *Something More* ... *Visit Dana Point, a headland between Laguna Beach and San Clemente, where Richard Henry Dana once dangled from a halyard to dislodge cowhides his companions had tried to throw to the beach below. Read Dana's account of his exploits in* Two Years before the Mast *(1840).*

HATFIELD THE RAINMAKER

n the early 1900s Southern California was in the midst of a severe drought. What it desperately needed was a rainmaker. Charles Mallory Hatfield seemed to be just the man for the job. To some folks Hatfield was a crackpot and a flimflam man, but to others he was a great pioneer meteorologist. Born in 1876, Hatfield developed an early penchant for dabbling in chemicals and concocting strange inventions. Soon after the turn of the century, he invented something he called a "moisture accelerator," a process which he claimed could make it rain.

Hatfield first demonstrated his invention in 1902 in Oceanside. Atop tall rainmaking towers, he placed evaporating tanks filled with a top-secret brew of foul-smelling, bubbling chemicals. Did Hatfield's invention work? Within five days, the city of Oceanside was blessed with more than one inch of rain, and Hatfield collected

from the city a handsome fee of fifty dollars. His fame soon spread throughout Southern California. Other communities began bidding for the services of Hatfield the Rainmaker.

Hatfield's biggest challenge came in San Diego in 1916. The city council agreed to pay Hatfield ten thousand dollars if he could fill the local reservoirs. Hatfield dutifully set up his rainmaking towers and mixed his noxious chemicals. Soon it began to rain—and it rained and it rained! The city's reservoirs filled to overflowing with some 18 billion gallons of water. Soon the city was flooded. Streets, highways, homes, and businesses were inundated. When it finally stopped raining, Hatfield dropped by the offices of the city council to pick up his "rain check." But the council refused to pay. They said they had hired Hatfield to fill the reservoirs *only*, not the whole darned city!

In time, Hatfield the Rainmaker fell from grace. Potential clients were afraid to hire him, fearing that his magic might work too well. As the drought ended, the need for a rainmaker quickly evaporated. Hatfield turned to other enterprises, spending his last years as a sewing-machine salesman in Glendale. There he died in 1958. To the chagrin of many drought-weary Californians today, Hatfield the Rainmaker kept his invention a secret. His "moisture accelerator" was lost forever.

> 🐚 *Something More* ... *View memorabilia of Hatfield and his invention at the Museum of the San Diego Historical Society, 1649 El Prado, San Diego 92101. Admission is $3.00. Hours are 10:00 A.M. to 4:30 P.M. Wednesday through Sunday. Telephone (619) 232-6203. Also visit the California Room, San Diego Public Library Central Branch, 820 E Street, San Diego 92101. Free. Hours are 10:00 A.M. to 9:00 P.M. Monday through Thursday, 9:30 A.M. to 5:30 P.M. Friday and Saturday. Telephone (619) 236-5800. The story of Hatfield the Rainmaker is wonderfully told in Richard Dillon,* Humbugs and Heroes: A Gallery of California Pioneers *(1970).*

THAT TENDER ABALONE

I f you've never savored a meal of California abalone, you really should give it a try the next time you're at your favorite seafood restaurant. Neptunian dining at its finest!

The abalone has been an important food source in California for thousands of years. Coastal California Indians prized the abalone not only for its delicious meat, but also for its beautiful iridescent, mother-of-pearl shell. The Chumash Indians along the Santa Barbara Channel decorated their ocean-going canoes with beautiful designs of inlaid abalone shells. They also fashioned abalone-shell fish hooks and beads to trade with tribes living further inland. When Europeans first arrived along the California coast, the Indians occasionally presented them with gifts of abalone—much as the Indians of New England brought the early colonists wild turkey and venison.

Unfortunately, today abalone is not as plentiful as it once was; the abalone population has been in serious decline for over thirty years. Some marine biologists blame the deteriorating water quality along the coast or rising ocean temperatures caused by *El Niño*. Some folks even blame the decline on the return of the sea otter, a natural predator of the abalone. It's not unusual these days to see these furry little critters floating on their backs, wrapped in kelp, contently dining on abalone on the half-shell. Whatever the cause, the California Department of Fish and Game recently imposed strict limits on abalone harvesting.

In the early 1900s, Carmel poet George Sterling wrote a song about the abalone. Sterling and his friends Jack London, Jimmy Hopper, and other California literati used to hold great abalone feasts on the beach at Point Lobos. They would gather around a roaring campfire and pound out the abalone meat to tenderize it. While pounding the abalone, each would contribute new verses to "The Abalone Song":

The Abalone Song

Oh some folks boast of quail on toast
Because they think it's tony
But I'm content to owe my rent
And live on abalone.

He wanders free beside the sea
Where ere the coast is stony.
He flaps his wings and madly sings
The plaintive abalone.

By Carmel Bay the people say
We feed the Lazzaroni
On Boston beans and fresh sardines
And toothsome abalone.

Some live on hope
And some on dope
And some on alimony.
But my tom cat he lives on fat
And tender abalone!

I've often thought how different American history would have been if the Pilgrims had landed at Carmel Bay instead of Plymouth Rock. Just think, we might never have stuffed a single turkey! Instead, all across the land, cooks would rise early on the morning of the third Thursday of November to pound their Thanksgiving abalone. Who knows, "The Abalone Song" might have become one of our nation's most beloved Thanksgiving carols. Ah, the glories of what might have been.

&*Something More* ... *View the fine collection of Chumash Indian artifacts made from abalone shells on display at the Morro Bay State Park Museum of Natural History off Main Street in Morro Bay 93442. Admission is adults $2.00 and children $1.00. Hours are 10:00 A.M. to 5:00 P.M. daily. Telephone (805) 772-2694. The story of "The Abalone Song" is told in Franklin Walker,* The Seacoast of Bohemia *(1966). Also read Fredric Hobbs,* The Spirit of the Monterey Coast *(1990) for a fascinating look at the growth of Monterey and Carmel.*

STELLA AT THE FAIR

an Francisco has hosted several grand expositions and world fairs, but none was finer than the great Panama Pacific International Exposition of 1915. Built on landfill in what is now the Marina District, the exposition celebrated both the opening of the Panama Canal and the recovery of the city from the earthquake and fire of 1906.

The PPIE, as the exposition was affectionately known, opened on the morning of February 20, 1915. San Francisco Mayor Jimmy Rolph led a procession of some 150,000 eager visitors onto the grounds amid shrieks of factory whistles, clanging cable car bells, and cannon booming from the Presidio. In a ceremonial flip of the switch in the nation's capitol, President Woodrow Wilson started the wheels turning in the Palace of Machinery and sent water gushing into the Fountain of Energy. Within nine months of opening day, the exposition had attracted some 18 million visitors.

Monumental buildings filled the grounds of the PPIE. Most impressive was the 435-foot Tower of Jewels, decorated with thousands of hand-cut multicolored Austrian glass crystals that glistened in the sun during the day and sparkled under a battery of searchlights at night. Today the only surviving building on the site is the Palace of Fine Arts (actually a replica of the original). Designed by Bernard Maybeck, the Palace housed over eleven thousand paintings never before seen in California.

The most popular area of the PPIE was known as the Zone. It featured a working model of the Panama Canal, a display of "Infant Incubators with Living Infants," and a talking horse named Captain. Most eye-catching of all was a fourteen-foot painting of a female nude called *Stella*. Viewed in a darkened room by gentlemen (mostly), Stella was said to be "of magnificent proportions." Her appeal was further enhanced by special effects that made her appear alive and breathing!

There is a sad irony to the PPIE. The exposition demonstrated magnificently the recovery of San Francisco from the 1906 earthquake. But its towering buildings and monuments stood on

unstable landfill created by dumping in the bay rubble from that earlier disaster. When the Loma Prieta earthquake struck in 1989, the heaviest damage in the city occurred in the Marina District, the very site of the great Panama Pacific International Exhibition.

> ❧ **Something More** … *Visit the picturesque temple of arches and columns that make up the Palace of Fine Arts, 3601 Lyon Street, San Francisco 94123. Free. The original gallery space is now the home of the Exploratorium, a collection of hands-on exhibits illustrating basic scientific principles, including plate tectonics and the origins of earthquakes. Admission is adults $6.00, children $2.00. Hours are 10:00 A.M. to 9:30 P.M. Wednesday and 10:00 A.M. to 5:00 P.M. Thursday through Sunday. Telephone (415) 563-7337.*

ADMISSIONS DAY

dmissions Day, the anniversary of the signing of the California Statehood Bill, used to be the occasion for parades and grand celebrations around the state. September 9 was a date dear to the heart of every child in California because for years it was a school holiday. Now we're apt to let the date pass unnoticed. That's a shame. California's admission to the union was an important event, not just for the state, but for the nation as well. Our admission as a free state intensified the sectional crisis between North and South. It brought the nation ever closer to Civil War.

Quick quiz: Can you name the president who signed the California Statehood Bill? Hint: San Francisco has a street and an entire district named in his honor. Although he doesn't otherwise rank among the great American leaders, it was Millard Fillmore who put pen to paper on September 9, 1850, approving California statehood.

News of this momentous event didn't reach San Francisco for about five weeks. On the morning of October 18, the *S.S. Oregon* sailed into San Francisco Bay with all flags flying in celebration of the exciting news it bore. The city went wild! All businesses and government offices closed. Folks rushed into the streets, shouting and firing guns in the air and waving flags. Soon a parade was organized down Market Street. City marshals in crimson scarves led the festivities, marching along with a brass band of buglers and a troupe of Chinese revelers carrying bright blue silk banners. That night, huge bonfires on Twin Peaks and other hills around the city lit the evening sky.

From San Francisco, the news was carried to neighboring towns. In breathless prose, a local observer described the excitement as the word was rushed to San Jose:

> Mounting his [wagon] behind six fiery mustangs lashed to their highest speed, the driver of Crandall's stage cried the glad tidings all the way to San Jose: "CALIFORNIA IS ADMITTED! CALIFORNIA IS ADMITTED!," while a ringing cheer was returned by the people as the [coach] flew by.

September 9, 1850, a date worth remembering—and celebrating!

> 🐦 *Something More* ... *For a highly entertaining account of San Francisco in the 1850s, see Doris Muscatine,* Old San Francisco: The Biography of a City from Early Days to the Earthquake *(1975). See also Robert G. Cowan,* The Admission of the 31st State by the 31st Congress *(1962).*

THE INTRIGUE OF *MCTEAGUE*

One of the most gripping novels ever written about San Francisco is Frank Norris's *McTeague*, the powerful story of a dentist totally corrupted by greed. Frank Norris was born in Chicago in 1870 and moved with his family to San Francisco when he was fourteen. The Norris home was on Sacramento Street, just a few blocks from the Polk Street neighborhood that later became the setting for *McTeague*. At age 17, Frank was sent to Paris to study art, but was soon summoned home by his father who suspected that young Frank was wasting both his time and money. Norris then enrolled at University of California, Berkeley, where he studied for four years but failed to graduate. (His old fraternity, incidentally, was Phi Gamma Delta. The brothers there still celebrate his birthday.)

After leaving college, Frank Norris became a professional writer in San Francisco and later in New York. His earliest success was the story of the evil Dr. McTeague who marries and then kills a young woman who has won a lottery prize of five thousand dollars. McTeague is pursued into Death Valley where he kills again. The brutal and sadistic dentist dies in the desert, handcuffed to his final victim's body.

Original manuscripts of important works such as *McTeague* usually end up in special libraries where they can be studied by scholars. In this case, the manuscript suffered an unusual fate. When publishers produced a new edition of *The Complete Works of Frank Norris* in 1928, they inserted one page of the original *McTeague* manuscript in each set of the volumes sold. This may have been a brilliant way to boost sales, but it hopelessly scattered the manuscript around the world. Years later, an English professor at the University of California, Berkeley, began an international search to recover the lost manuscript. Eventually about 40 percent of the *McTeague* pages were located and are available now for study at the university's Bancroft Library.

McTeague seems to have all the makings of a blockbuster motion picture—a great plot, strong characters, and a tantalizing mixture of sex and violence. In 1924, the great German director Eric von Stroheim became fascinated with the story of *McTeague*. Working for MGM, von Stroheim shot every scene on all 447 pages of the book. His faithfulness to the original text was admirable, but created something of a problem. The completed movie consisted of forty-two reels of film and ran for ten hours! MGM ordered von Stroheim to begin cutting. The director worked for six months and managed to reduce the film to less than five hours. Still MGM was not satisfied, so they cut it even more. When the film, entitled *Greed*, was finally released, it was a financial disaster. Von Stroheim was so outraged by the butchering of his masterpiece that he refused ever to see it!

&⬥ Something More ... *Visit the San Francisco neighborhood that was the setting for McTeague. The area is known as Polk Gulch, nestled in between Pacific Heights and Nob Hill, and is bordered by Sacramento, Polk, Sutter, and Van Ness streets. The Norris home is at 1822 Sacramento Street. One of the earliest (and still the best) biographies of Frank Norris is Franklin Walker,* Frank Norris *(1932).* Greed *is occasionally shown at the Pacific Film Archive, 2625 Durant Avenue, Berkeley. Admission is $5.00. Discounts available for children and students of University of California, Berkeley. Telephone (415) 642-1412 and for a recording of upcoming screenings (415) 643-5041. In the Los Angeles area, the film may also be seen at UCLA's Film and Television Archive Department, Melnitz Theatre, Melnitz Hall, 405 Hilgrad Avenue, Los Angeles 90024. Admission is $3.00 with discounts for students and seniors. Telephone (213) 206-3456 for upcoming screenings.*

LEGEND AND LORE
OF LAKE TAHOE

here's always been some dispute about the origin of the name Tahoe, but apparently it's a Washo Indian word meaning "big water" or simply "lake." The first name chosen by Anglo-Americans was Lake Bonpland, to honor a French botanist named Aimé Bonpland, but that never really caught on. (I guess it just didn't sound right to say, "I'm going up to Bonpland for the weekend.") In the early 1850s, the lake was named Lake Bigler after the Democratic governor of California, John Bigler. Later, when the Republicans took over, the name was changed again. Some suggested a made-up Indian name. How does Lake Tula Tulia sound? Fortunately that didn't catch on either. It wasn't until 1945 that the name Lake Tahoe was officially adopted by the legislature. This, of course, created something of a redundancy since "Lake Tahoe" is best translated as "Lake Lake."

My favorite Lake Tahoe legend is about a couple of San Francisco businessmen who went fishing one day on the lake back in the 1860s. The men supposedly discovered a great hole at the bottom of the lake through which water drained into the nearby silver mines. The men developed an ingenious device to plug and unplug the drain, thus allowing them to manipulate the price of silver mining stock in San Francisco. When they unplugged the drain, the mines would flood and prices of silver mining stock would plummet. The businessmen would then buy up stock at dirt-cheap prices. When they plugged the hole, the mines would drain and stock prices would skyrocket. The businessmen then would sell out their stock and make a fortune!

Of course all this is just a tall tale, but it's been repeated so many times that a lot of folks think it really happened. Even today, I've been told, you can still find people out there on the lake looking for that "great drain of Lake Tahoe."

ह Something More ... *Hire a boat at one of the many lakeside vendors at Lake Tahoe and try your hand at finding that mythical drain. Or visit the Gatekeeper's Cabin Museum, operated by the North Lake Tahoe Historical Society, 130 West Lake Boulevard, Tahoe City 96145. Free. Hours are 11:00 A.M. to 5:30 P.M. Telephone (916) 583-1762. Read some of the other colorful stories inspired by Lake Tahoe in Edward B. Scott,* Sagas of Lake Tahoe *(1973).*

I'LL HAVE THE CARP, PLEASE

We rarely think of the great English writer Aldous Huxley as a Californian, yet he lived in the Golden State for the last quarter century of his life. Huxley first visited California in the 1920s as a young man and moved permanently to Los Angeles in 1938, after gaining international fame for his masterpiece, *Brave New World*.

Aldous Huxley moved to Southern California for several reasons. Initially he was attracted by the prospect of working in Hollywood as a screen writer. Indeed, he did manage to make some good money working on films such as *Pride and Prejudice* and *Jane Eyre*. Huxley also moved to Los Angeles—and this seems rather quaint today—because of its reputation for clean air! Huxley had contracted an eye disease early in life, and the crisp, clean atmosphere of the Southland was reputedly good medicine.

California proved to have a profound impact on Huxley's later career. He was influenced by its fascination with the culture and philosophy of the Far East and by the newly emerging drug culture. He began experimenting with LSD and mescaline in the early 1950s and described his experiences in an intriguing underground classic called *The Doors of Perception* (1954).

Aldous Huxley's most important California book was *After Many a Summer Dies the Swan* (1939), a satire based loosely on the life of William Randolph Hearst. Invoking considerable literary license, Huxley transposed Hearst Castle from San Simeon south to the San Fernando Valley and populated the estate with a band of Steinbeckian Okies working as serfs in the castle's orange groves. The story tells of an aging California millionaire's futile quest for eternal youth. When he discovers that carp have been known to live for two hundred years or more, the hopeful lord of the manor takes up a youth-preserving diet made up entirely of raw carp guts!

Aldous Huxley died on November 22, 1963, the same day President John F. Kennedy was assassinated. News of Huxley's death in California was understandably overshadowed by other events of the day.

ॐ Something More ... *Read Aldous Huxley's fictional account of the Hearst Castle in* After Many a Summer Dies the Swan *and compare it with the real thing at the William Randolph Hearst State Park, located on Coast Highway 1, San Luis Obispo 93452. Tour fees start at $12.00 and are given throughout the day. Summer hours are 8:00 A.M. to 5:00 P.M.; winter hours are 8:20 A.M. to 3:20 P.M. Telephone (800) 444-7275 for reservations and directions.*

BUMMER AND LAZARUS

O f all the eccentrics whose stories are a part of California history, perhaps none is more revered than Joshua Abraham Norton, a hard-driving businessman who made and then lost a fortune in the years following the California gold rush. Sadly, when Norton's money went so did his mind. He took on a new identity and began calling himself "Norton the First, Emperor of the United States and Protector of Mexico." San Francisco indulged Norton's fantasy; he was accepted as something of an unofficial city mascot. Emperor Norton became a familiar sight on the city streets, dressed in a gold-braided frock coat, an elaborate hat of plumed ostrich feathers, and a ceremonial sword at his side. In restaurants, the Emperor's meals were always complimentary. When he did need money, he simply cashed checks drawn on his "Imperial Government Treasury."

The story of Emperor Norton has become so embellished over the years it's now almost impossible to separate fact from fiction. One of my favorite Emperor Norton yarns is the shaggy dog story of Bummer and Lazarus. According to local legend, Bummer and Lazarus were two stray curs who somehow became a part of the Emperor's royal entourage. The origin of Bummer's name is lost in the mists of time, but apparently Lazarus was christened because of his miraculous return from the dead. Bummer one day discovered his partner lying half-dead in a Montgomery Street alley, brought him bits of food, and nursed him back to health.

How these two unlikely characters became associated with Emperor Norton is not altogether clear, but once they latched on to the Emperor they were his constant companions. According to local tradition, it was not uncommon to see the smiling, tail-wagging twosome attending the theater with the Emperor on opening nights in special reserved seats. They were seen together at the synagogue on Saturday mornings; on Sundays they faithfully attended mass at St. Mary's church.

Accounts of the demise of Bummer and Lazarus are a bit more reliable. When Lazarus met his tragic end under the wheels of

a fire truck, San Francisco's newspapers printed tearful eulogies. Thousands of mourners attended a grand public funeral to pay their last respects. Bummer died a couple of years later of old age. The papers carried his obituary too, but because old Bummer had begun neglecting his personal habits he had fallen somewhat from public favor. Mark Twain was one of those who mourned Bummer's passing:

> The old vagrant Bummer is really dead at last, and although he was always more respected than his obsequious vassal, the dog Lazarus, his exit did not make half as much stir in the newspaper world as signalized the departure of the latter. I think it is because he died...full of years, and honor, and disease, and fleas.

🐾 **Something More** ... *Read the fascinating story of this quintessential San Francisco character and his companions in William Drury,* Norton I, Emperor of the United States *(1986). Also read Malcolm E. Barker,* Bummer and Lazarus: San Francisco's Famous Dogs *(1984).*

STRAWBERRY POINT
AND THE UNITED NATIONS

hen most of us think of the United Nations, we picture its world headquarters standing alongside the East River in Manhattan. Imagine, for a moment, what it would be like if that gleaming glass and steel high-rise stood instead on Marin County's Strawberry Point. Farfetched? Not at all, for there once was a very real possibility that the United Nations would be located in Marin County, not Manhattan. This should be no surprise to those who remember that San Francisco was, after all, the birthplace of the United Nations.

The idea for the United Nations began near the end of World War II when the great Allied leaders, Roosevelt, Churchill, and Stalin, agreed that a meeting should be held to establish a new world organization. The proposed conference was imperiled by the death of Roosevelt just thirteen days before it was to begin. The crisis passed when Harry Truman, in one of his first official acts as president, announced that the meeting would be held as scheduled. On April 25, 1945, the "United Nations Conference on International Organization" convened in San Francisco.

California Governor Earl Warren issued a warm welcome to the delegates from the fifty nations represented at the conference. For the next several months, the delegates and their staffs filled the Fairmont, the Mark Hopkins, and many of the other grand hotels of the city. The meeting took place at the War Memorial Opera House in the Civic Center. The formal signing of the United Nations Charter was a spectacular event, marked by all the glitter and pomp of an opening night at the opera. The stage was adorned with flags from the fifty member nations as each of the delegates came forward to sign the charter.

United Nations officials gave serious consideration to locating the new organization in California. They investigated the possibility of purchasing a parcel of land on Strawberry Point in Marin County. However, John D. Rockefeller, Jr., intervened and made the

United Nations an offer it couldn't refuse. He donated $8.5 million to the organization for its permanent headquarters with only one, very clear stipulation: the United Nations must be located in New York City.

I've always thought that the United Nations missed a real bargain here in the Golden State. Not long after the organization decided not to buy the land at Strawberry Point, the property was sold to the Golden Gate Baptist Theological Seminary for a mere four hundred thousand dollars. Since then, the property has increased enormously in value. Recently seventeen acres were put on the block for a cool $13.2 million!

&**Something More** ... *Visit the site of the United Nations Conference at the War Memorial Opera House, 301 Van Ness Avenue, San Francisco 94102. Tours of the Opera House as well as of the Herbst Theatre and Louise M. Davies Symphony Hall are available Mondays only (excluding holidays) between 10:00 A.M. and 2:30 P.M. Tours start at the Davies Symphony Hall box office, corner of Van Ness and Grove. Tour fee is adults $3.00, students and seniors $2.00. Telephone (415) 552-8338. The proposed location for the headquarters of the United Nations may be viewed at the Golden Gate Baptist Theological Seminary, Seminary Drive, Strawberry Point, Mill Valley 94941. Free. Hours are 9:00 A.M. to 4:00 P.M. Tours can be arranged by calling (415) 388-8080, ext. 275.*

BECKWOURTH
OF BECKWOURTH PASS

Jim Beckwourth was one of that reckless breed of men who once roamed the Far West in search of adventure. He was a mountain man and frontier scout who dressed in fringed buckskins and beaded moccasins. He wore his long black hair braided Indian-style over his shoulders; around his neck hung a pendant made of a rifle bullet and two brightly colored oblong beads.

Born in Virginia in 1798, Jim Beckwourth's father was a plantation owner and his mother a black slave. At his earliest opportunity, Beckwourth escaped from the Deep South and headed for the freedom of the West. For a while, he was adopted by the Crow Indians and lived with them along the Yellowstone and Bighorn rivers. He later became a Crow warrior, eventually serving as a chief of the tribe. Among the Snake Indians, he was known as "Bloody Arm" because of his prowess in battle. Make no mistake about it, Jim Beckwourth was a tough character.

Jim Beckwourth drifted into California during the gold rush and prospected around Murderer's Bar and then up on the Feather River at Rich Bar. There he was discovered by an itinerant journalist who was fascinated by Beckwourth's stories. The journalist noticed that Beckwourth's eloquence increased in inverse ratio to the diminishing supply of rum. Therefore, he made sure that Beckwourth was well supplied with rum, and Beckwourth saw to it that the journalist was well supplied with stories.

By the time Jim Beckwourth reached California, he was already well established as one of the great black pioneers of the West. Somewhere along the line, he also developed into quite an entrepreneur. In 1851, Beckwourth discovered the pass through the northern Sierra Nevada that now bears his name. Because the route had excellent commercial possibilities, the citizens of Marysville agreed to pay Beckwourth to build a toll road over the pass. Jim spent about sixteen hundred dollars of his own money building the

road and succeeded in guiding the first immigrants across. The townfolk of Marysville were so pleased with Beckwourth they held a grand celebration. Unfortunately, the partying got a little out of hand, and half the town burned down! The fire also destroyed the assets of Beckwourth's backers, who then rather sheepishly informed him that they could cover only a couple hundred dollars of his expenses. Needless to say, Jim Beckwourth was none too pleased.

> ?❧ **Something More** ... *Travel across Beckwourth Pass, east from Portola on Highway 70. Visit Beckwourth's newly restored cabin, three miles east of Portola on Rocky Point Drive. Telephone the Marysville Chamber of Commerce (916) 743-6501 for more information. A good biography is Elinor Wilson,* Jim Beckwourth *(1972).*

THE NOB HILL STORY

ob Hill in San Francisco has long been a symbol of the city's elegance and grace. Known originally as the California Street Hill, in the 1870s it became the home of San Francisco's wealthiest families. They were called "nabobs," a term which originated during the early days of the British Empire when the local elite in India were the "nawabs." In San Francisco, the name was shortened simply to "nobs"; hence, "Nob Hill."

On the crest of the hill were the homes of the Big Four, the men who had made their fortunes building and running the Central Pacific and Southern Pacific railroads. The home of Leland Stanford was on California Street where the Stanford Court Hotel stands today. Visitors to the magnificent Stanford home entered through a circular entrance hall, bathed in amber light from a glass dome in the ceiling seventy feet above. Guests were expected to pass reverently across the gleaming floors with their black marble inlays of the signs of the zodiac, which Mrs. Stanford, a dedicated spiritualist, took very seriously. From there guests entered a formal reception room decorated in the style of the East Indies and then progressed toward the grand sitting room which was draped with purple and gold velvet in the manner of royalty.

Mark Hopkins lived up the street and, compared to the other members of the Big Four, was a fairly simple and unpretentious sort. His wife Mary Ellen, on the other hand, exuded lavish taste. Their home, where the Mark Hopkins Hotel stands today, was incredible. Topped by a crown of towers, gables, and steeples, it looked like a medieval castle. Inside were drawing rooms fashioned after the Palace of the Doges, a dining room paneled in carved English oak that could seat sixty, and a master bedroom decorated with ebony and ivory and ornamented with jewels and semiprecious stones.

Charles Crocker's home was the grandest of them all, occupying an entire square block where Grace Cathedral stands today. Crocker's 12,500-square-foot home contained a fully equipped theater, library, and billiard room. If that weren't enough, an imposing

seventy-six-foot tower offered Crocker an uninterrupted view of the entire Bay Area.

The view was not so grand for Crocker's neighbor, a lowly San Francisco undertaker named Yung who had refused to sell out when Crocker was buying up the block for his new residence. To spite the uncooperative Mr. Yung, Crocker constructed a fence forty-feet high on three sides of his neighbor's property! The Crocker "spite fence" became a familiar attraction in the city, a galling symbol of the unrestrained wealth and power of these nabobs of old San Francisco.

Each of these lavish homes was destroyed in the great earthquake and fire of 1906. The epitaph for such earthly mansions can be found in Ecclesiastes. "Vanity of vanities," warns the preacher, "all is vanity."

&**Something More** ... *View the fine collection of photographs of the homes that once festooned the top of Nob Hill while dining in elegance at the Big Four Restaurant in the Huntington Hotel, 1075 California Street, San Francisco 94108. Telephone (415) 474-5400 for reservations. The most readable account is Oscar Lewis's classic,* The Big Four *(1938).*

GAM SAAN

O f all the diverse peoples who have contributed to the rich multiethnic history of California, perhaps none has been more fascinating—and more often misunderstood—than the Chinese. Most people are familiar with the stereotypical image of the Chinese launderer working away in some remote gold country mining camp. Like most stereotypes, this really doesn't give us a very accurate picture of historical reality. The Chinese did come to California during the gold rush, but they came primarily to mine gold, *not* to wash clothes. In fact, by 1870 approximately one-fourth of the miners in California were Chinese. News of the gold discovery had spread rapidly throughout China, and California had become known as a fabulous land—*Gam Saan* or "Gold Mountain."

Unfortunately the Chinese immigrants often received a hostile reception in California. Many Anglo-American workers opposed the Chinese because of their willingness to accept low wages. Much of the opposition was based on essentially irrational fears directed against a foreign people whose way of life was thought to be somehow dangerous to the well being of the state. Anti-Chinese riots broke out in cities and towns throughout California in places like Auburn, Petaluma, Roseville, Chico, Santa Barbara, and Los Angeles.

Cities also passed laws to harass the Chinese. In 1870, for instance, San Francisco passed an ordinance prohibiting anyone from occupying a sleeping room with less than 500 cubic feet of breathing space per person. This "health law" allowed the police to make raids on crowded Chinatown tenements and roust out any sleeping Chinese residents who might be violating the ordinance while they slept. The law was vigorously enforced and soon the jails of San Francisco were so overcrowded that the city itself was in gross violation of its own ordinance!

In spite of such opposition, the Chinese made many positive contributions to California and the West. Thousands of Chinese laborers worked for the Big Four to build the first transcontinental railroad. Chinese railworkers were suspended in wicker baskets over sheer granite cliffs to chisel out a ledge for the tracks across the Sierra Nevada. Chinese immigrants also built hundreds of miles of reclamation levees in the Sacramento delta, dug caves for wineries in the Sonoma and Napa valleys, and fished for shrimp and abalone in Monterey Bay.

The Chinese also made a major contribution to California horticulture, both as farm laborers and farm owners. One reminder of this contribution is something you can see each summer in the supermarket. It's the Bing cherry, named after a Chinese farmer on the West Coast named (believe it or not!) Ah Bing.

❧ Something More ... Visit the Museum of the Chinese Historical Society of America, 650 Commercial Street, San Francisco 94111. Free. Hours are 12:00 noon to 4:00 P.M., Tuesday through Saturday. This exciting museum contains the largest collection of Chinese-American artifacts in North America. Telephone (415) 391-1188. For an excellent introduction to the subject, read Him Mark Lai et al., The Chinese of America, 1785–1980 *(1980).*

RICHMOND AT WAR

he largest shipbuilding complex in the world was once located in the San Francisco East Bay city of Richmond. The Kaiser Shipyards, named after their founder Henry J. Kaiser, produced the legendary Liberty ships that played such a key role during World War II.

At the beginning of the war, Kaiser Shipyards was assigned the task of building ships at a rate faster than the Germans or Japanese could sink them. Displaying the "can do" spirit so typical of wartime America, the shipyard rose to the challenge. Thousands of employees were soon working around the clock, at night under huge floodlights, to build the vital ships. By 1943, the average keel-laying-to-launching time for a Liberty ship was a mere twenty-seven days! An all-time record of 4 days, 15 hours, 26 minutes was set with the launching of the Liberty ship *Robert E. Peary.*

Before the war, Richmond was a small town of about twenty four thousand people. By 1945, it was a booming industrial city of over one hundred thousand. This phenomenal growth was a mixed blessing. It put a tremendous strain on the city's ability to provide basic services. Shortages were soon evident in everything from schools to sewers. Rooming houses sprang up, offering what were called "hot beds." These were beds rented to shipyard employees who worked different shifts throughout the day and night. As one worker left for work, another would arrive; thus the bed was always "hot." Transportation was another big headache for Richmond. Old electric railcars from the New York City Elevated were put into commuter service along San Pablo Avenue. Outdated ferry boats were dug out of the mud, refitted, and once again shuttled workers across the bay.

For the shipyards, the biggest problem was the labor shortage. With so many able-bodied men going off to war, Henry J. Kaiser launched a massive recruiting effort to tap new sources of labor. He advertised for workers in every part of the country, offering such inducements as high wages, on-the-job training, and a subsidized plan for group medical care. The response to this appeal was overwhelming. Thousands of black workers arrived from the South, seeking the extraordinary opportunities for high-paying jobs now open to them in the shipyards. Likewise, women throughout the country responded. They joined the Kaiser shipyard workforce and enjoyed a degree of economic independence previously denied them. The image of "Rosie the Riveter" captured the nation's imagination.

A marvelous symbol of those tumultuous times in Richmond was a huge sign that stood at the entrance to the Kaiser Shipyards. It said "Help Wanted!!! Male or Female, Young or Old, Experienced or Inexperienced!" With great imagination, but perhaps not too much exaggeration, someone added "Dead or Alive!!!"

&❧ *Something More* ... *Tour the* Jeremiah O'Brien, *the one remaining seaworthy Liberty ship open to the public. It is docked at Pier 3 at the Fort Mason Center, corner of Bay and Laguna streets, San Francisco 94123. Admission is adults $2.00, children $1.00. Hours are 9:00 A.M. to 3:00 P.M. daily. Telephone (415) 441-3101. The story of wartime Richmond is placed in broad historical context in Gerald D. Nash,* The American West Transformed: The Impact of the Second World War *(1985).*

THE GOOPS
AND THE PURPLE COW

> The Goops they lick their fingers
> And the Goops they lick their knives;
> They spill their broth on the tablecloth—
> Oh, they lead disgusting lives....

The Goops, in fact, were little bald-headed, rubber-limbed cartoon characters created in the 1890s by a talented young San Franciscan named Gelett Burgess. Member of a prominent New England family of *Mayflower* lineage, Burgess arrived in California in 1888 and went to work as a draftsman for the Southern Pacific Railroad. After three years of life in California, Burgess was transformed. He discovered that his true passion in life was writing poetry, not designing railroads.

Rejuvenated by his newfound identity, Gelett Burgess plunged into the Bohemian life of San Francisco. He and a dozen other young writers and artists began calling themselves *Les Jeunes* (the young ones) and emulated their heroes Robert Louis Stevenson and Oscar Wilde. Burgess took on a flamboyant personal style, wearing an unconventional knee-length cape, festooned each day with a fresh carnation in his lapel. Quick-witted and highly energetic, Burgess was the central figure in this coterie of young talent.

Gelett Burgess achieved international fame for his poem "The Purple Cow." You may remember it.

> I never saw a Purple Cow,
> I never hope to see one
> But I can tell you anyhow
> I'd rather see than be one!

The poem first appeared in *The Lark*, a literary magazine founded in 1895 and edited by Burgess. The immense popularity of the poem eventually caused Burgess to regret ever having written it. He considered himself a serious poet and was exasperated at always

TABLE MANNERS.—I.

THE Goops they lick their fingers,
   And the Goops they lick their
      knives;
They spill their broth on the table-
      cloth—
   Oh, they lead disgusting lives!
The Goops they talk while eating,
   And loud and fast they chew;
And that is why I'm glad that I
   Am not a Goop—are you?

being identified with that one silly little poem. Yet "The Purple Cow" was typical of the material published in *The Lark*. Its mood was always whimsical; it never pretended to be anything serious.

After two years of successful publication, boasting some three thousand subscribers, the popularity of *The Lark* declined. In its final issue, Gelett Burgess had just one thing to say about that "Purple Cow."

> Ah, yes, I wrote the "Purple Cow"—
> I'm Sorry, now, I wrote it;
> But I can tell you Anyhow,
> I'll Kill you if you Quote it!

❧ Something More ... *Read collections of Gelett Burgess's early San Francisco writings in* Bayside Bohemia *(1954) and* Behind the Scenes *(1968). For the further adventures of the Goops, see Burgess's* Goops and How to Be Them *(1900).*

THE HUNGARIAN FATHER
OF CALIFORNIA WINE

he California wine industry began back in the days of the Spanish missions when the Roman Catholic padres and their Indian wards planted the first vineyards. From all reports, this mission wine was pretty poor stuff. It wasn't until the early American period in the 1850s that commercial wine production in California became successful. Much of that success was due to a colorful character known as the father of California viticulture, "Count" Agoston Haraszthy.

Haraszthy migrated from his native Hungary to the United States in 1840. He was a man with a passion for growing grapes. He planted his first vineyard in Wisconsin, where (fortunately for the future of California agriculture) most of his vines froze during the first winter. He next came to San Francisco and tried again, but his grapes failed to ripen because of the all too-familiar summer fogs.

In 1856, Haraszthy moved north to the Sonoma Valley. Here at last he found a place where conditions were ideal for growing grapes. He built the famed Buena Vista Winery, complete with lime-

stone caves, beautiful formal gardens, and sparkling fountains. A rivalry developed between Haraszthy and his grape-growing neighbor in Sonoma, Mariano Vallejo. However, it must have been friendly because Haraszthy's two sons, Arpad and Atilla, married two of Vallejo's daughters!

Haraszthy was sent to Europe in 1861 by the state of California to import more grape varieties and to study winemaking. He returned with over one hundred thousand cuttings of some three hundred different varieties of grapes, including the first California tokays and zinfandels. But somehow the state never got around to paying Haraszthy for his trip. Eventually he left California in disgust.

Haraszthy ended up on a sugarcane plantation in Nicaragua, where he hoped to make rum for the export trade. One fateful day, according to some accounts, he tried to cross a swollen stream on his plantation by walking across a tree limb. As luck would have it, Haraszthy tripped, fell into the stream, and was promptly eaten by alligators!

> ɜ∿ *Something More* ... *Visit the Buena Vista Winery, a State Historic Landmark, at 18000 Old Winery Road, Sonoma 95476. Free self-guided tours are available from 10:00 A.M. to 5:00 P.M. daily. Telephone (707) 938-1266. See also Leon D. Adams,* The Wines of America *(1990).*

RALSTON OF THE PALACE

illiam Chapman Ralston was one of the wealthiest San Franciscans in the late 1800s, a man of tremendous drive and ambition. He was president of the Bank of California and made millions from investments in Comstock silver mines. He later expanded his fortune through large real estate developments in the Bay Area.

Ralston lived in a lavish villa in Belmont on the San Francisco Peninsula. Among his many distinguished visitors was the American ambassador to China, Anson Burlingame. It was in honor of Ambassador Burlingame that Ralston named one of his nearby developments. His greatest enterprise in San Francisco was the grand Palace Hotel which opened in 1875. Guests could drive their carriages into the elegant Palm Court, a room six stories high, and be greeted by uniformed footmen.

At the peak of his power and prestige, Ralston overextended himself and suffered a major financial collapse. A run on the Bank of California forced the institution to close its doors. The next day, the bank directors asked for and obtained Ralston's resignation. Later that afternoon, Ralston went for his daily swim in the bay and never made it back to shore. A few hours later his body was recovered.

One of the many California monuments to the memory of William Ralston is the town of Modesto. In his salad days, Ralston made a sizeable loan to one of the directors of the Southern Pacific Railroad. When the Southern Pacific built lines through the San Joaquin Valley, the railroad wanted to name a town in his honor. Ralston said thanks, but no thanks. Frankly he didn't want his name associated with some raw new town in the valley. Instead, the railroad directors bestowed the honor indirectly by naming the town Modesto, after Ralston's presumed modesty. But everyone knew that Ralston had an enormous ego. Naming the town Modesto was really a grand and glorious inside joke!

&**Something More** ... *Visit the Garden Court restaurant in the Sheraton Palace Hotel, Market and New Montgomery, San Francisco 94105. The Garden Court is a replica of the original Palm Court which once graced Ralston's Palace Hotel, destroyed in the 1906 earthquake and fire. Telephone (415) 392-8600 for reservations. Ralston's residence on the Peninsula may be viewed on the campus of the College of Notre Dame, 1500 Ralston Avenue, Belmont 94001. Fees for docent-led tours are adults $3.00, students and seniors $2.00. Reservations must be made in advance. Telephone (415) 508-3501. Ralston's story is well told in David Lavender's biography,* Nothing Seemed Impossible: William C. Ralston and Early San Francisco *(1975).*

SARAH WINCHESTER'S FIXER-UPPER

arah Pardee Winchester, widow of millionaire William Winchester and heiress of the vast Winchester Rifle Company fortune, lived a life of tragedy and mystery. Shortly before her husband succumbed to tuberculosis, her only child died in infancy. Sarah Winchester never escaped the shadow of these two devastating losses.

Grief-stricken, but wealthy beyond belief, Sarah Winchester in 1884 purchased an eight-room farmhouse near San Jose. With her inheritance of over $20 million, and a dividend income of one thousand dollars a day, she hired a small army of carpenters to begin expanding and remodeling her little house.

Sarah Winchester insisted that only the finest materials be used. She imported exotic hardwoods from around the world and placed huge orders for crystal and chandeliers of gold and silver. The total cost of her project eventually exceeded $5.5 million. Sarah Winchester was its sole architect. She met with her foreman every morning to show him what she had planned during the night. Rooms were built, built around, and ripped out as she saw fit. Her completed fixer-upper had forty-seven fireplaces, one hundred sixty rooms, two thousand doors, and ten thousand windows!

Much about Sarah Winchester remains a mystery. In her old age she became increasingly reclusive, forbidding anyone from even taking her photograph. Chief among the mysteries is the question of Sarah's motives. According to some accounts, a psychic told her that to atone for the millions of deaths caused by the Winchester rifle she must devote her life to the building of a lavish structure. The psychic warned Sarah that if she stopped building, she would surely die. Others say that Sarah built the house with its repeating patterns of thirteen and its ten thousand windows so that spirits of the departed could float freely in and out. Another explanation is that Sarah's mind was unsettled by the personal tragedies she suffered early in life.

Whatever her motives, Sarah Winchester kept her staff of carpenters at work for nearly forty years. It wasn't until her death in 1922 that the hammers and saws in the house of Sarah Winchester finally fell silent.

> ❧ **Something More** … *Visit the Winchester Mystery House, 525 South Winchester Boulevard, San Jose 95128. Admission is adults $10.95, seniors $8.75, children $5.95. Guided tours available 9:00 A.M. to 4:00 P.M., Monday through Friday and 9:00 A.M. to 4:30 P.M. Saturday and Sunday. Telephone (408) 247-2101. The best time to visit the house is on Halloween when flashlight tours are presented 7:00 P.M. to 11:00 P.M. (You even get to keep the flashlight!)*

THE ATHERTONS OF ATHERTON

he founding Atherton of Atherton was Faxon Dean Atherton, a Massachusetts-born merchant who made a fortune in Chile. In 1860, Atherton and his Chilean-born wife moved to the San Francisco Peninsula where they bought a five-hundred-acre estate, built a lavish villa called Fair Oaks, and lived for many years in the grand manner of the landed gentry. After Faxon's death in 1877, his estate became the town of Atherton.

Another prominent Atherton was Faxon's son George, inheritor of much of the family fortune. As a young man, George courted a twice-divorced older woman in San Francisco, Mrs. Gertrude Horn. The courtship ended soon after George met her eighteen-year-old daughter, a blond, blue-eyed beauty also named Gertrude. She and George promptly fell in love and eloped—much to the chagrin of George's former sweetheart who now was his mother-in-law!

Theirs was a stormy relationship. Gertrude blossomed into a successful writer, eventually producing nearly sixty books. Among her most popular works were romantic California histories, *Before the Gringo Came* (1894) and *The Splendid Idle Forties* (1902). She also was an outspoken feminist. Some of her novels and essays were powerful critiques of domesticity and the subjugation of women. One of her later novels, *The Sophisticates* (1931), included sensational scenes of the rejuvenation of older women. Meanwhile, George was becoming increasingly possessive and intensely jealous of his wife.

After ten years of fractious marriage, George Atherton sailed to Chile. A few days out at sea, he died of a ruptured kidney. His body was packed in a barrel of rum and shipped back to the family in California. According to popular legend, the barrel arrived at the Athertons' home where an unknowing butler popped the lid to get at the rum and was shocked to find his master floating inside!

৯০ Something More … *Read* The California Diary of Faxon Dean
Atherton *(1964). Also read the story of Gertrude Atherton in her
own words,* Adventures of a Novelist *(1932). A remarkable new
biography is now available, Emily Wortis Leider,* California's
Daughter: Gertrude Atherton and Her Times *(1991).*

THE WORLD'S GREATEST WRITER

illiam Saroyan was a creative genius who made his mark as a novelist, a short story writer, and a playwright. Born to an Armenian immigrant family in Fresno in 1908, Saroyan dropped out of school at age twelve.

As a struggling young writer, William Saroyan developed a flamboyant persona. There was always something about him that seemed larger-than-life. He sported a drooping, handlebar mustache and unabashedly billed himself as "The World's Greatest Writer." Saroyan's first big hit was a collection of twenty-six short stories called *The Daring Young Man on the Flying Trapeze*, written in 1934 at the rate of one story a day. At the time, Saroyan was living in a furnished room on Carl Street in San Francisco near Golden Gate Park. The title story is about a day in the life of a young writer who has nothing to eat and is completely destitute except for one penny that he finds on the sidewalk!

One of Saroyan's most successful works was a play written in 1939 entitled *The Time of Your Life*. It tells the story of a group of down-and-outers befriended at a San Francisco bar by a wealthy drunk who gives them all some money to pursue their dreams. The bar in the play was Nick's Waterfront Saloon, based on Saroyan's favorite San Francisco hangout, Izzy Gomez's Saloon in North Beach.

William Saroyan made his big money as a Hollywood screenwriter working for Louis B. Mayer at MGM. He won an Oscar for his 1943 screenplay, *The Human Comedy*. (Recently the statuette appeared in a San Francisco pawn shop, having been pawned for $250.) Three years earlier, Saroyan was awarded a Pulitzer Prize for *The Time of Your Life*. Upon receiving the award, he turned down the thousand-dollar prize money. He said the money should go to some truly needy writer. Yet Saroyan himself was often in debt, and he was criticized by his family for mishandling his finances. Saroyan vigorously defended his spending habits, pointing out that he always managed to buy the essentials: "I drank some of it away, and I bought a raincoat."

> 🎗️ **Something More** ... *Visit the site of William Saroyan's apartment at 348 Carl Street, San Francisco 94117. A collection of Saroyan memorabilia, including his "wandering Oscar," is displayed at the Fresno Metropolitan Museum, 1555 Van Ness Avenue, between Calaveras and Stanislaus streets, Fresno 93721. Admission is adults $2.00, children and seniors $1.00. Hours are 11:00 A.M. to 7:00 P.M. Wednesday through Sunday (Wednesdays are a free day!) Telephone (209) 441-1444.*

HISTORY 680

Long before Highway 680 through Alameda and Contra Costa counties was choked with traffic and strewn with shopping malls, this Bay Area commuter corridor was a well-traveled thoroughfare.

It started out as a footpath, a trail used by California Indians on trading expeditions hundreds of years ago. Later came Spanish priests and soldiers who traversed the path in the late 1700s. Their diaries describe the surrounding hills covered with golden fields of wild oats. Eventually the route was known as the Old Spanish Trail and became a favorite passageway for forty-niners heading from the San Francisco Bay Area to the southern mines of the Sierra Nevada.

One of the familiar place names along that route today is the town of Sunol, named for Antonio María Suñol, a young Spanish sailor who came to California aboard a French naval vessel in 1818. Suñol jumped ship in Monterey, married the daughter of a wealthy *Californio* family, and was granted a vast rancho in southern Alameda County. His ranch house, with its lush gardens and shaded patio, became a favorite stopover for travelers along what is now Interstate 680.

Contrary to what you might expect, the nearby town of San Ramon was not named after a saint. The name honors an old sheep-herder who once lived out that way and whose name happened to be Ramon. The "San" was tacked on years later, probably by some well-meaning local booster, to match all the other Spanish place names in California.

One of the first settlers along the future route of Interstate 680 was a true native Californian, José María Amador, born in San Francisco in 1794. (To keep this date in perspective, remember that in 1794 the President of the United States was George Washington.) When Amador was a young man, he received a rancho grant of six-teen thousand acres of prime East Bay real estate—land enough for him to support his large and growing family. Amador eventually married three times and claimed to have fathered some thirty-seven children!

After the Mexican War and the discovery of gold in 1848, most of the *Californios* lost their lands to the newcomers. Amador was able to sell most of his rancho estate, at quite a bargain price, to an Irish-American named James Witt Dougherty. Dougherty paid twenty-two thousand dollars for Amador's adobe ranch house and over ten thousand acres of land. The area then became known as Dougherty's Corners. Later two Irishmen, Michael Murray and Jeremiah Fallon, bought some property nearby. "There are so many Irishmen out here," Dougherty once said, "you might as well call this place Dublin." And so it came to be.

> ❧ ***Something More*** ... *Visit Dublin's Heritage Center, a cluster of historic buildings just off of Dublin Boulevard in Dublin. St. Raymond's Church (1859) has a well-preserved pioneer cemetery. Adjacent is the old Murray School, which houses the museum of the Dublin Historical Preservation Association, 6600 Donlan Way, Dublin 94568. Free. Hours are 1:00 P.M. to 5:00 P.M. Sundays. Telephone (415) 828-3377. A good book on Dublin is Virginia Bennett,* Dublin Reflections *(1978). Also a useful reference book is Barbara and Rudy Marinacci,* California's Spanish Place-Names *(1988).*

THE SHAFTS AND BATHS
OF ADOLPH SUTRO

ere's a story of a man who started on top and dug his way down to a fortune. Adolph Sutro had an amazing ability to make money, a talent he proved time and time again.

Born in Prussia in 1830, Adolph Sutro immigrated to the United States when he was just twenty years old. After a brief stop in Baltimore, he headed out to San Francisco. From there he was off to the Comstock silver mines. As a self-trained mining engineer, Sutro had conceived a brilliant and daring plan for a revolutionary new way of mining the Comstock.

Sutro's proposal was to dig a massive tunnel to strike the center of the silver lode directly beneath Virginia City. The new tun-

A. Hendrick

nel would provide superior access to the mines and offer improved ventilation and drainage for the miners. After raising over $6.5 million from eager investors, Sutro ordered the digging to begin. When the tunnel was completed in 1869, it was the longest tunnel in the world. The main shaft was ten feet high, twelve feet wide, and a phenomenal three miles long. It reached a depth of 1,650 feet, three times deeper than any tunnel before. Sutro made a fortune with his tunnel by contracting for its use at a rate of two dollars per ton of ore mined.

In 1879, Adolph Sutro sold his interests in the tunnel and turned to investing in San Francisco real estate. Eventually he owned one-twelfth of all the property in the city. His vast domain included lands stretching from the top of Sutro Heights (adorned today with that red-eyed monster, Sutro Tower) all the way out to the ocean beach. One of his largest parcels was a thousand-acre estate overlooking Seal Rocks. There he built a magnificent home and gardens.

Nearby Sutro constructed an elaborate Victorian hotel and restaurant, the Cliff House, and built the Sutro Baths. The baths were enormous. They could accommodate ten thousand swimmers in six huge glass-enclosed pools, each at a different temperature, ranging from 50 to 110 degrees. There were palm-studded decks and promenades, as well as galleries where up to three thousand spectators could stroll and observe the bathers below. When the Sutro Baths opened in 1896, a full day of swimming and promenading cost only ten cents!

&*Something More* ... *Enjoy a Sunday brunch at the Cliff House, that cozy but rather modest establishment which replaced Adolph Sutro's more elaborate structure destroyed by fire in 1907. Located at 1090 Point Lobos, San Francisco 94121. Hours are 9:00 A.M. to 10:30 P.M. daily. Telephone (415) 386-3330. All that remains of the Sutro Baths are its crumbling concrete foundations, visible north of the Cliff House. For the full story of this dynamic California entrepreneur, see Robert E. and Mary F. Stewart,* Adolph Sutro *(1962).*

THE GREAT DIAMOND HOAX

One day in 1871, two grizzled prospectors strolled into San Francisco's Bank of California. When Philip Arnold and John Slack reached the teller's window, they produced a buckskin bag and asked to have it placed in the bank's safe. The teller peered inside the bag and saw it was filled with sparkling diamonds and what appeared to be sapphires, rubies, and emeralds. News of this unusual deposit soon reached the bank's president, the financial wizard William Chapman Ralston.

Ralston sent word that he'd like to have a little chat with the two new depositors. When Arnold and Slack met with Ralston they revealed they'd discovered a fabulous diamond mine. Ralston expressed great interest. Mindful of the simple beginnings of the California gold rush and the more recent Comstock silver rush, Ralston speculated that a diamond rush was about to begin. He envisioned developing an American diamond industry that would put its South African and European competitors out of business.

The two prospectors were cautious. They would show the mine to a representative from the bank, but only if they could take him there blindfolded. Ralston agreed. When the bank's representative saw the mine, he was dazzled. There were diamonds everywhere! When Ralston got the good news, he persuaded the two prospectors to accept $600,000 for a share in the mine.

After completing his deal with Arnold and Slack, Ralston received a second opinion. The noted geologist Clarence King visited the mine and became suspicious when he discovered that none of the diamonds were embedded in rock. He found them lying in the dirt, in an ant hill, and even resting in tree trunks! When King found one diamond already cut and polished, he was convinced the mine was a hoax. King sent word to Ralston immediately, but it was too late. The two prospectors were long gone and so too was Ralston's $600,000. For Philip Arnold and John Slack there had been a diamond rush indeed!

> 🐚 *Something More* ... *Read the full story of the great diamond hoax in George Dunlop Lyman,* Ralston's Ring *(1937) and David Lavender,* Nothing Seemed Impossible *(1975).*

NOT THE BOAR FLAG

The California state flag commemorates an event that occurred nearly 150 years ago. On Sunday morning, June 14, 1846, a band of some thirty rough-hewn American frontiersmen descended upon the Sonoma home of General Mariano Guadalupe Vallejo. This was back in the days when California was still a part of Mexico, and Vallejo was a prominent Mexican leader.

The Americans surrounded General Vallejo's *casa grande* and informed him that he was a prisoner of war. Vallejo politely

invited a few of his captors inside, served them some of his best brandy, and asked them to please explain just what war he was a prisoner of. The Americans proudly proclaimed that theirs was a war for the independence of California. Meanwhile, in front of Vallejo's house, the rebels hoisted a flag emblazoned with a crude drawing of a bear, a lone star, and the words "CALIFORNIA REPUBLIC."

Although the Bear Flag Revolt, as this incident came to be called, is a revered part of California history, I've always thought of the California Republic as more myth than reality. After all, how large was this so-called republic? Not much larger than the little village of Sonoma. Certainly the rest of California was never under the control of the Bear Flaggers. And how long did the republic exist? Less than a month. The regular armed forces of the United States invaded California in early July and launched a military conquest of what was still a Mexican province. What countries recognized the existence of the California Republic? None. The Bear Flag Revolt is a colorful incident, but its historical importance can easily be overstated.

The original Bear Flag, by the way, was quite different from our modern state flag. The original was made by William Todd, nephew of an up-and-coming young Illinois attorney named Abraham Lincoln. Todd used a three-by-five foot piece of white cotton cloth. Along the bottom he sewed several strips of red flannel taken from either a man's shirt or a woman's petticoat. He then painted a five-pointed red star in the upper left-hand corner. Using blackberry juice and brick dust, he wrote beneath the star the fateful words "CALIFORNIA REPUBLIC." As a final touch, he drew a picture of a California grizzly bear. But William Todd clearly was no artist. His grizzly looked more like a pig than a bear—but we know it must have been a bear because, most assuredly, this was *not* the Boar Flag Revolt!

&❧ *Something More* ... *Visit the Bear Flag Monument on the town plaza in Sonoma. A replica of the original "piggish" bear flag is on display at the nearby Sonoma Barracks, corner of First Street East and East Spain Street, Sonoma 95476. Admission is adults $2.00 and children $1.00. Hours are 10:00 A.M. to 5:00 P.M. daily. Telephone (707) 938-1519. An excellent account of the events surrounding the Bear Flag Revolt appears in Neal Harlow,* California Conquered: War and Peace on the Pacific, 1846–1850 *(1982).*

INDEX

Note: Historic sites, museums, and other points of interest are shown in bold type.

Note: Historic sites, museums, and other points of interest are shown in bold type.

Note: Historic sites, museums, and other points of interest are shown in bold type.

Ives, Burl, 48

J

Japanese, 86
Jeremiah O'Brien, 87
***Jeremiah O'Brien* Liberty Ship, San Francisco**, 87
Les Jeunes, 88
Jones, Commodore Thomas ap Catesby, 46–47
Jordan, David Starr, 2

K

Kaiser Shipyards, 86–87
Kaiser, Henry J., 86
Kalloch, Isaac, 8–9
Kennedy, John F., 74
King, Clarence, 106
KFSG, 42

L

La Beata, 45
La Pérouse, Jean François Galaup de, 14
Lake Tahoe, 72–73
The Lark, 88
Lassen County, 80–81
"Last Will and Testament," 49
Lazarus, 76–77
LeFranc, Charles, 15
"letter sheet," 39–41
Les Jeunes, 88, 90
Liberty ships, 86–87
Lincoln, Abraham, 8, 108
Lincoln Park, 9
Loma Prieta earthquake, 67
London, Jack, 63
Long Day's Journey Into Night, 48
Los Angeles, 6, 42–43, 62, 74, 84
Los Gatos, 57–58

Louise M. Davies Symphony Hall, San Francisco, 79
Lucas Valley, 48

M

M. H. de Young Museum, San Francisco, 9
Mariposa County, 41, 51–52
Marin County, 25–26, 48, 78–79
Marina District, 66
Mark Hopkins Hotel, 78, 82
Martínez, Doña María, 25
Marysville, 80–81
Marysville Chamber of Commerce, Marysville, 81
Marx, Karl, 27
Massachusetts, 2
Masson, Paul, 15
Matisse, Henri, 18
Maybeck, Bernard, 66
Mayer, Louis B., 99
Mazeppa, 22
McCarthy, Martin, 58
McCarthysville, 58
McPherson, Aimee Semple, 42–43
McTeague, 70–71
Menken, Adan Isaacs, 22
Mexican War, 47, 102
Mexico, 38, 46, 57
MGM, 71
Mill Valley, 25
mining, 84, 101, 103
"The Miner's Ten Commandments", 39–41, 51
Mission Dolores, 4, 25
mission wine, 91
missions, 4, 25–26, 91
Mississippi, 6
Miwok Indians, 51
Modesto, 94
"moisture accelerator," 61
Monterey, 46–47, 101

Note: Historic sites, museums, and other points of interest are shown in bold type.

Note: Historic sites, museums, and other points of interest are shown in bold type.

Note: Historic sites, museums, and other points of interest are shown in bold type.

Note: Historic sites, museums, and other points of interest are shown in bold type.

Warren, Earl, 78
Washington, George, 101
Wells Fargo, 16–17
Wells Fargo History Museum, San Francisco, 17
Wesley Hotel, Niles, 36
whaling, 25
Wilde, Oscar, 88
William Randolph Hearst State Park, San Luis Obispo, 75
William Richardson Adobe Home Site, San Francisco, 26
William Saroyan's Apartment, San Francisco, 100
Wilson, Woodrow, 66

Winchester Mystery House, San Jose, 96
Winchester, Sarah Pardee, 95
wine industry, 14–15, 91–92
Wisconsin, 91
women, 2, 4–5, 12–13, 18–19, 20, 22, 25, 34, 42–43, 44–45, 48, 82, 87, 95–96, 97
Wright, William, 22–24

Y

Yosemite, 51–52
Yosemite National Park, Yosemite, 41, 51–52
Yuba County, 80–81

Note: Historic sites, museums, and other points of interest are shown in bold type.

Other Tioga Books You Will Enjoy

The Spirit of the Monterey Coast
Fredric Hobbs

A prominent artist uses words and his illustrations to comment on the essence of the creative forces of philosophers, photographers, artists, and writers who have made this timeless coastline their home and inspiration.
 Photographs. Original line drawings. Index. 122 pages. Hardcover $24.95.

San Francisco Bay Area Landmarks
Reflections of Four Centuries
Charles Kennard
Foreword by James D. Houston

Handsome duotone photographs and historic quotations bring alive the stories of the land and people around the Golden Gate. The author/ photographer, British-born and architect-trained, presents the beauty of the natural scene and the architectural "marks" on the land.
 Photographs. Index. Bibliography. 160 pages. Hardcover. Special price $19.95.

Passing Farms: Enduring Values
California's Santa Clara Valley
Yvonne Jacobson
Foreword by Wallace Stegner

This handsome volume filled with old photographs is a nostalgic flashback to the early days of "the Valley of Heart's Delight," now known as Silicon Valley.
 Photographs. Color plates. Index. 250 pages. Hardcover. $29.95

California's Spanish Place-Names
Barbara and Rudy Marinacci

Here is a very useful resource—a compilation of stories about towns and cities with Spanish origins. It illustrates in an informal style Hispanic influence on the growth of California. You will use it also as a travel companion.
 Drawings. Index. Dictionary. 267 pages. Softcover $9.95

These books may be purchased at your favorite bookstore. Or send a check and include 8% tax and $1.50 per book for postage and handling. Or note your Visa/Mastercard number, expiration date, and provide your signature.

Tioga Publishing Company
Box 50490
Palo Alto, CA 94303
415-965-4081